AF575933

# GREATER PORTLAND

## PORTLAND, MT. HOOD, AND THE COLUMBIA GORGE

BARBARA TRICARICO

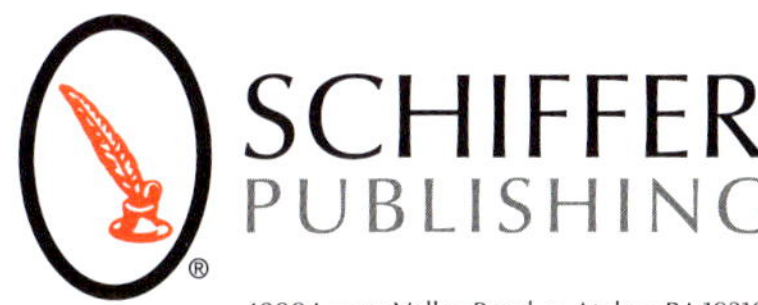


4880 Lower Valley Road • Atglen, PA 19310

**Other Schiffer Books by the Author:**
*Oregon Coast*, ISBN 978-0-7643-5947-7
*Southern Oregon*, ISBN 978-0-7643-5948-4
*Central Oregon*, ISBN 978-0-7643-5945-3



Library of Congress Control Number: 2020943528



Designed by Molly Shields
Cover design by Danielle Farmer
Front cover photo by Clem Paslack
Back cover photos by Terry Tuttle and Vivian McAleavey

Type set in BentonSans/Cambria

ISBN: 978-0-7643-6159-3
Printed in China

Published by Schiffer Publishing, Ltd.
4880 Lower Valley Road
Atglen, PA 19310
Phone: (610) 593-1777; Fax: (610) 593-2002
E-mail: Info@schifferbooks.com
Web: www.schifferbooks.com

# INTRODUCTION

When travelers decide to visit Oregon, they normally think of well-known Portland first. The city is the largest in the state and has approximately 632,309 residents, almost two-thirds of Oregon's total population. Its territory became widely known thanks to Lewis and Clark's journey in 1805.

Just outside the bustling city of Portland is an incredibly scenic region: the Columbia River Gorge. The Gorge is frequently regarded as one of the top ten drives in America. Along the drive you'll see dozens of picturesque waterfalls, including everyone's favorite, the mighty Multnomah Falls.

Framed like a postcard from almost any viewpoint within a hundred miles is majestic Mount Hood. The 11,250-foot mountain is the state's highest volcano and the second-most-climbed mountain in the world, boasting eleven glaciers. Mount Hood was named one of the Seven Wonders of Oregon by *Travel Oregon*. It is the only ski area in North America open all year long.

The historic Timberline Lodge was built and furnished by local artisans during the Great Depression and is now a national historic landmark.

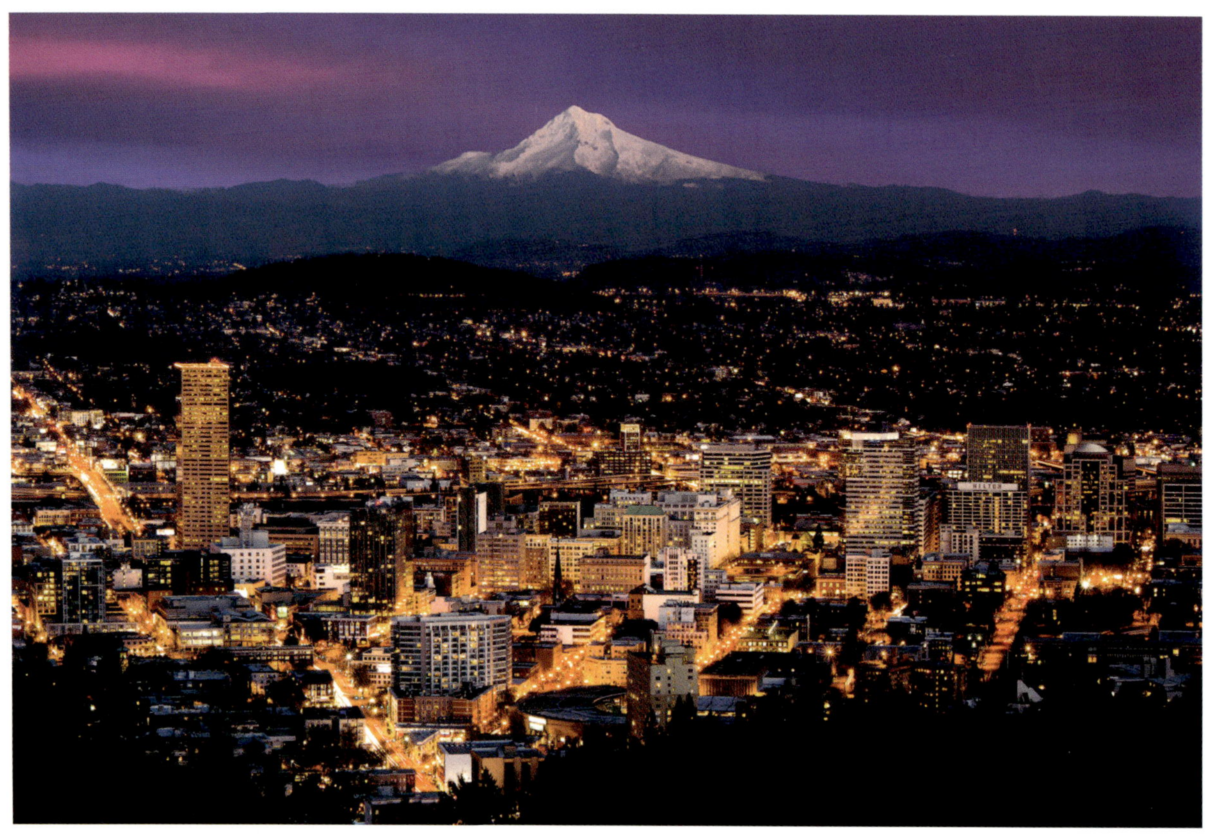

View of Mount Hood and downtown Portland from Pittock Mansion. *Photo by Clem Paslack*

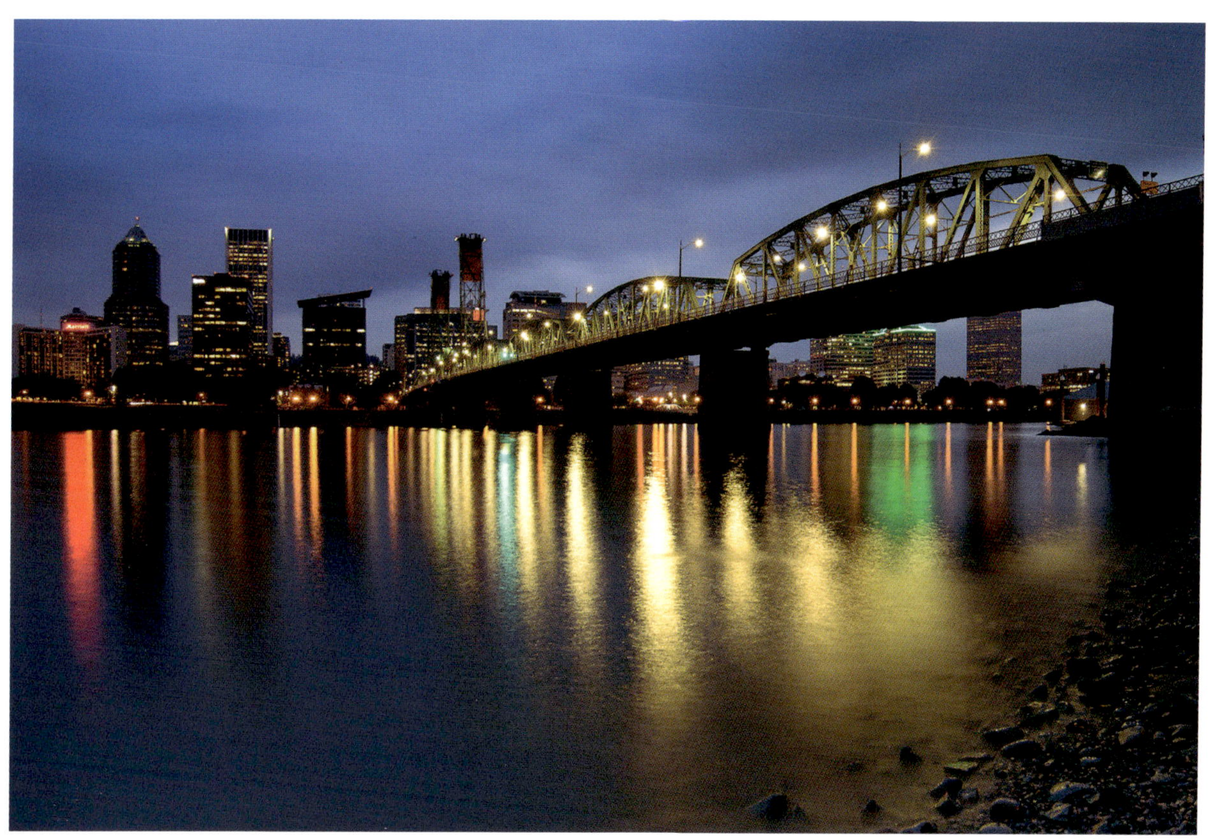

Hawthorne Bridge at the blue hour. *Photo by Clem Paslack*

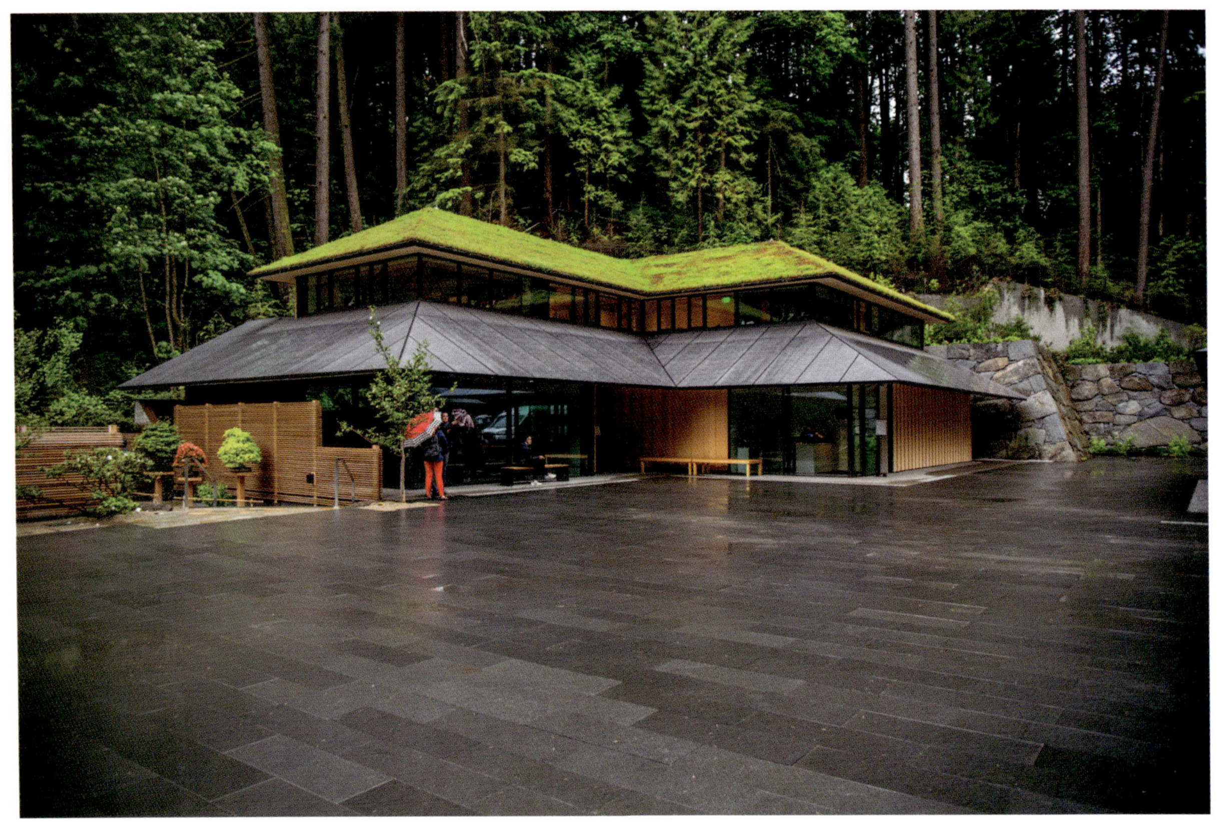

Japanese Garden Cultural Village. *Photo by George F. Peterson*

Portland Japanese Garden. *Photo by Barbara Tricarico*

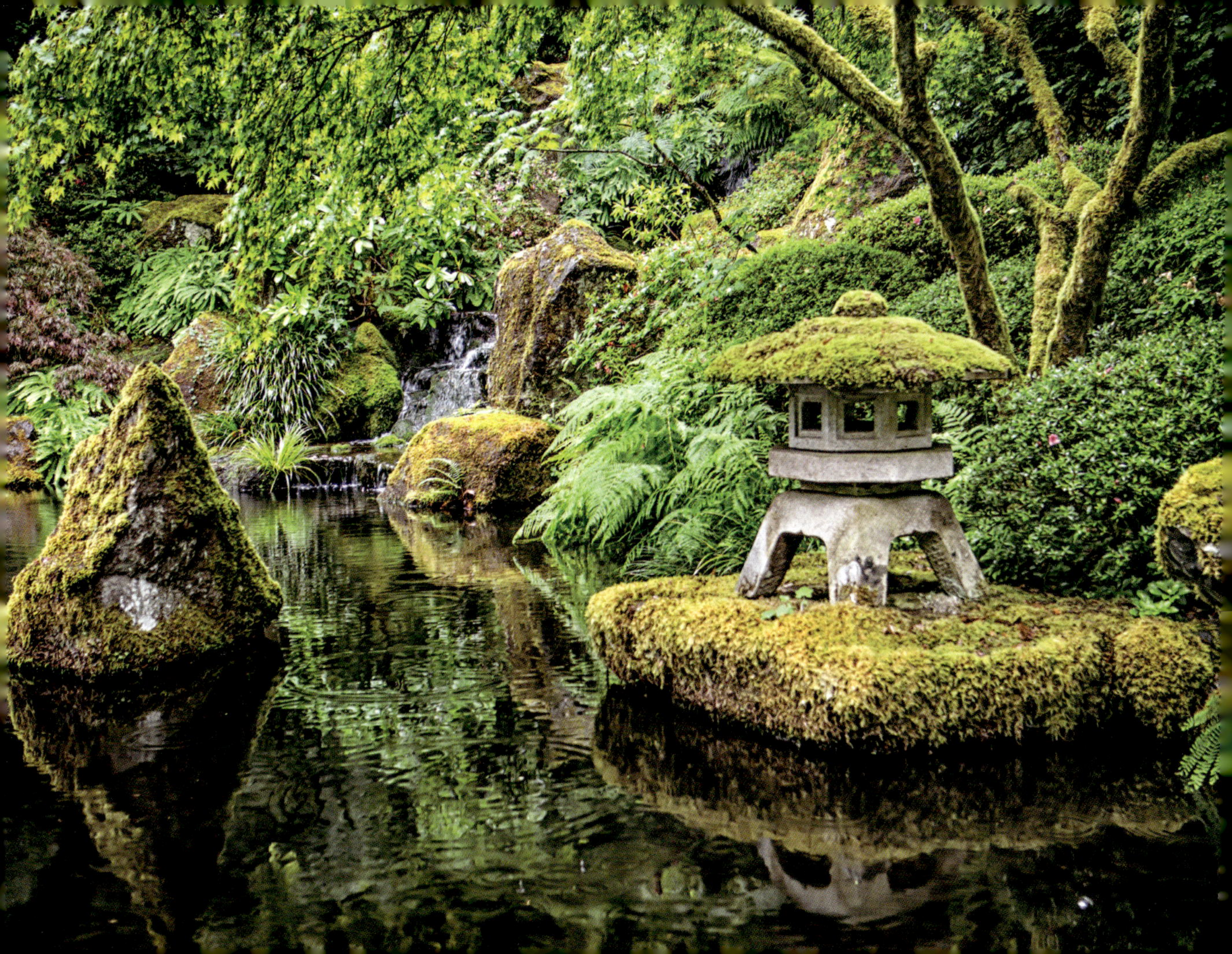

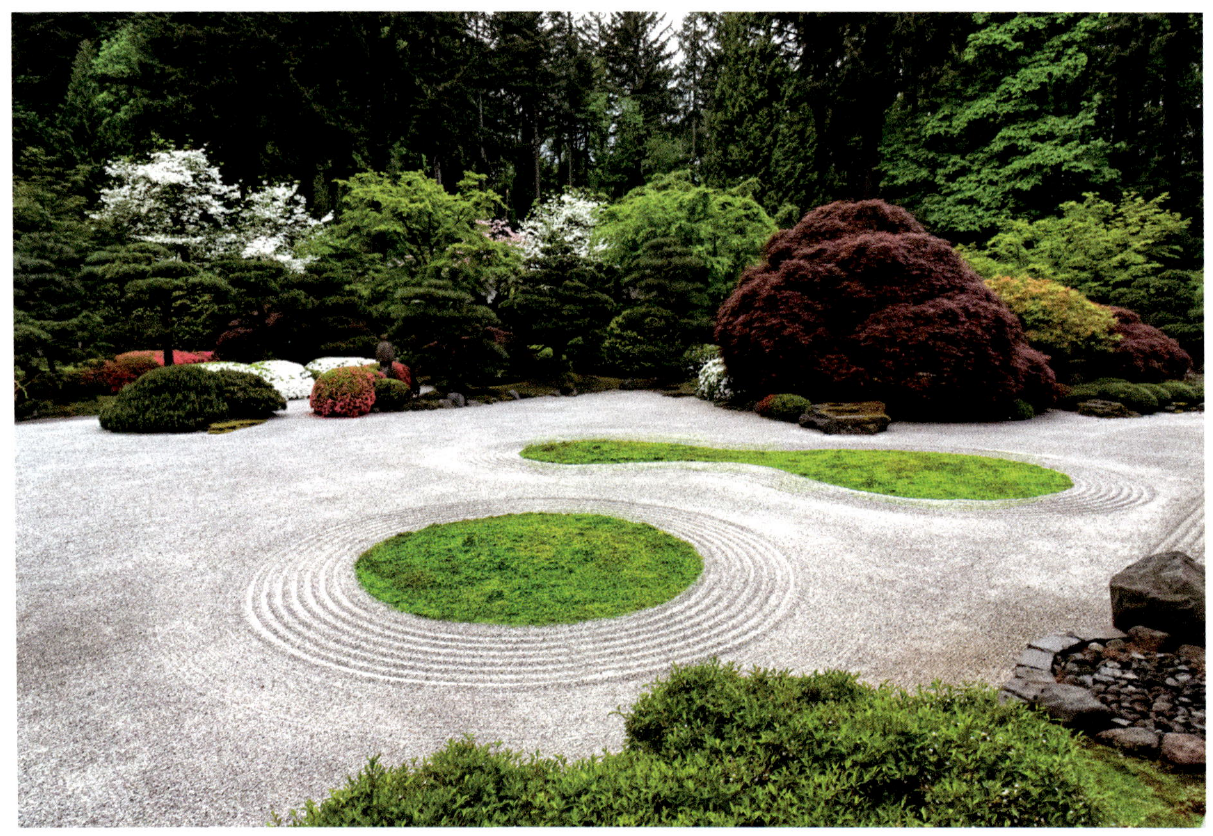

Sand and Stone "Karesansui" garden, Portland Japanese Garden.
*Photo by Barbara Tricarico*

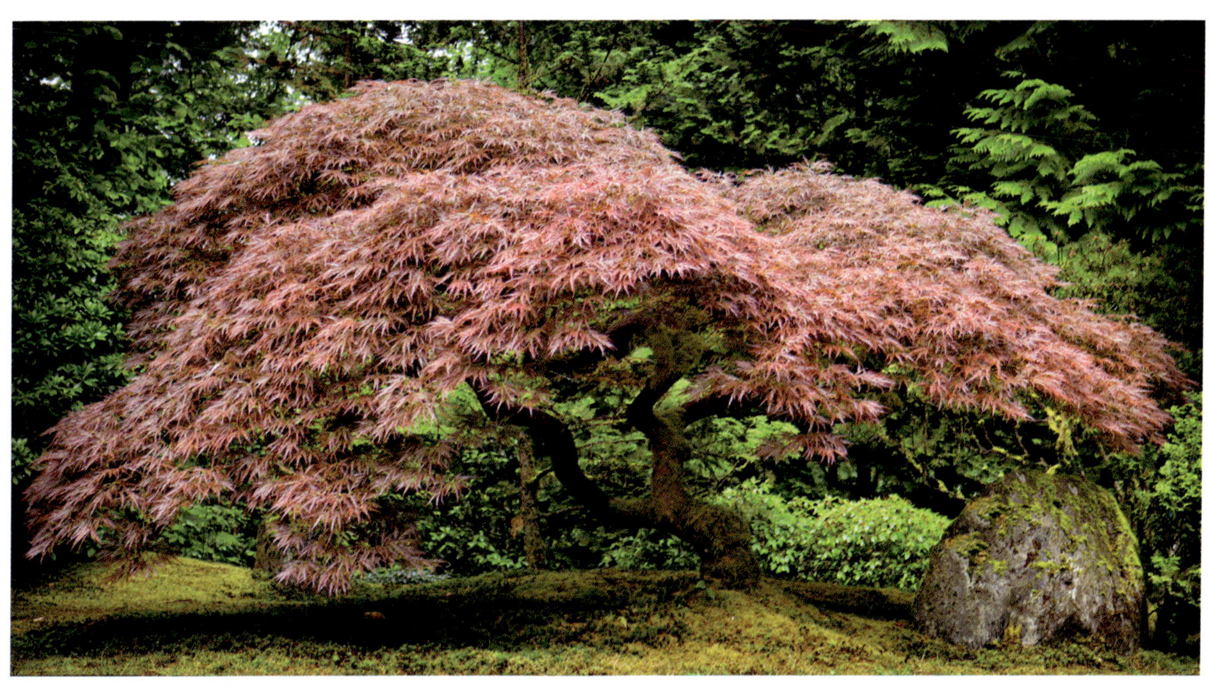



Japanese maple tree in Portland Japanese Garden.
*Photo by Barbara Tricarico*

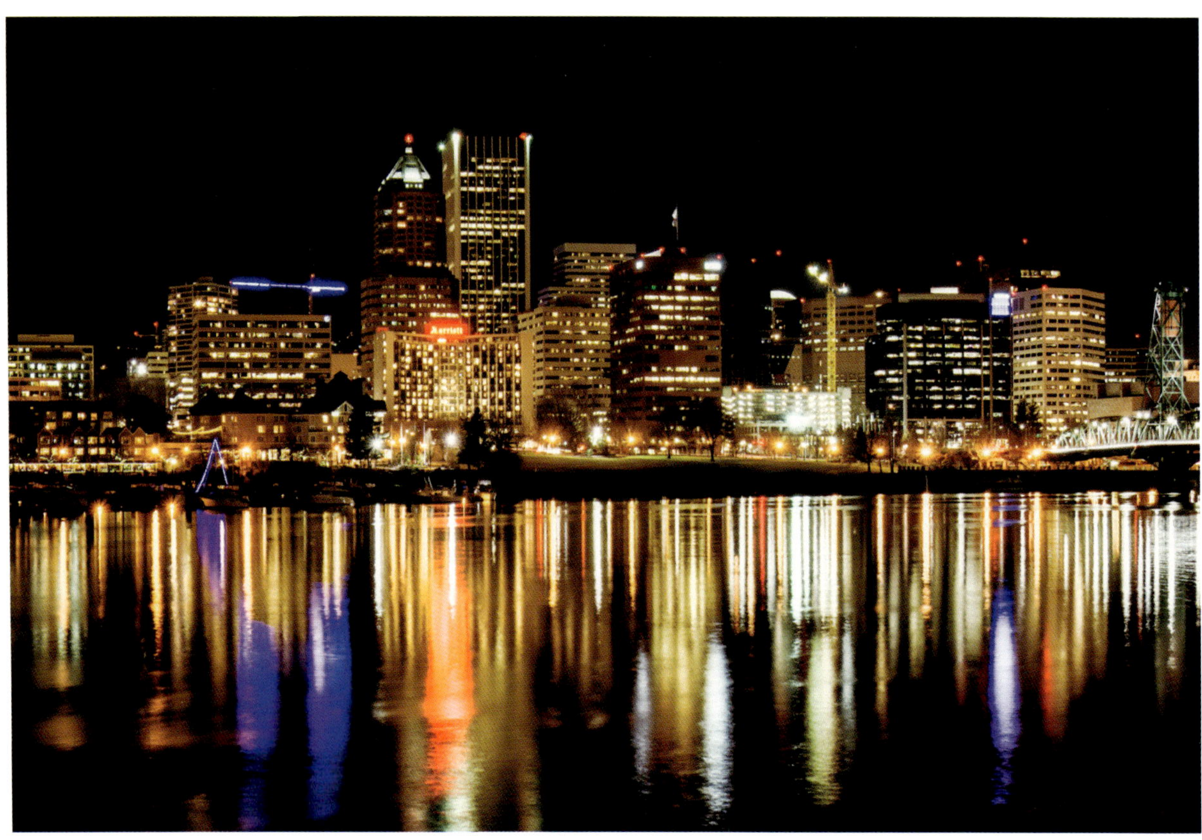

Portland skyline at night. *Photo by Barbara Tricarico*

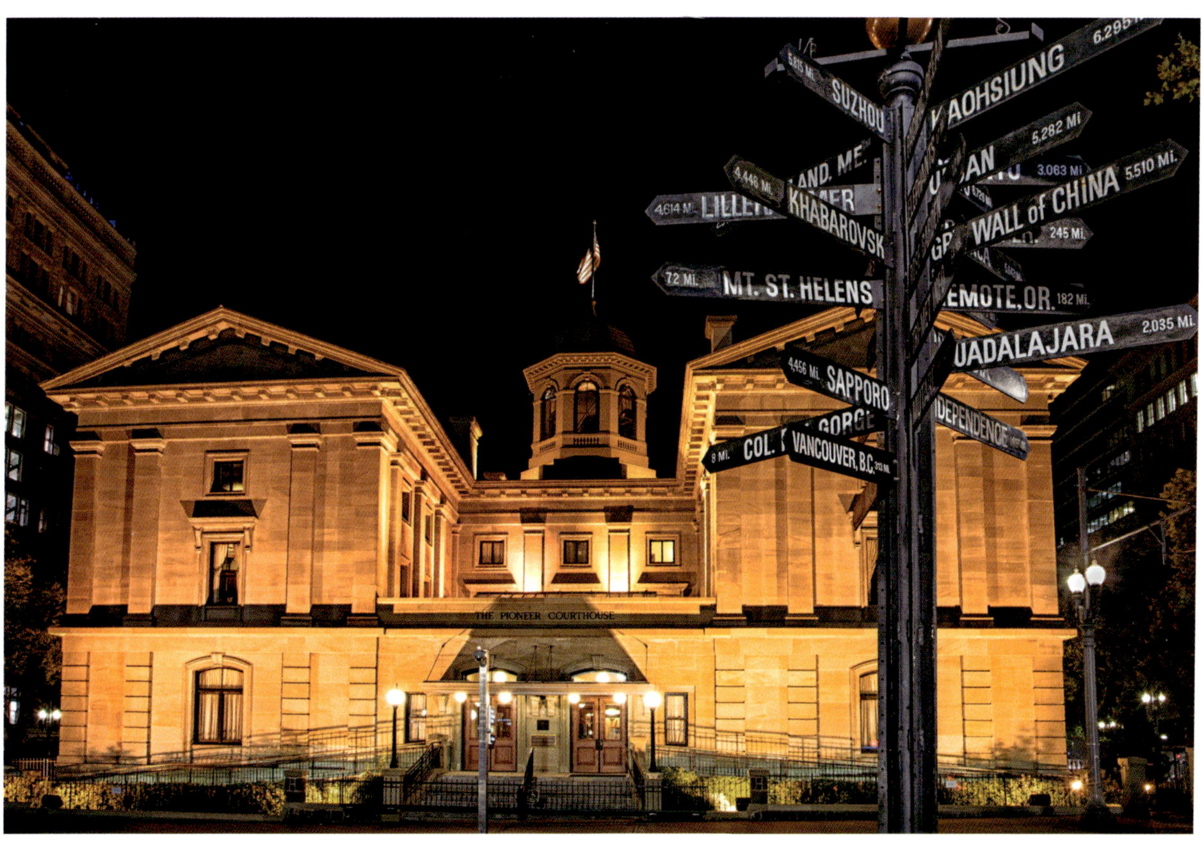


Pioneer Courthouse, built in 1869, and milepost sign.
*Photo by Barbara Tricarico*

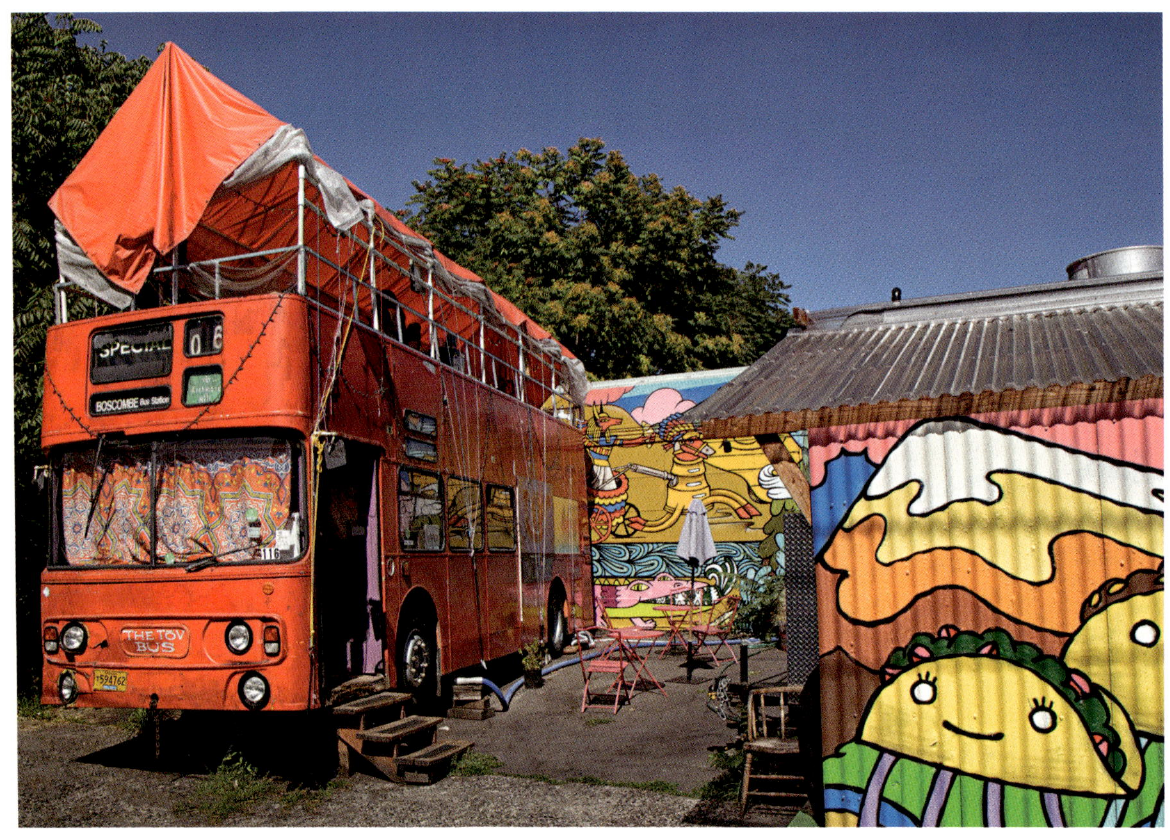


The double-decker Tōv Coffee Shop bus in Portland.
*Photo by Barbara Tricarico*

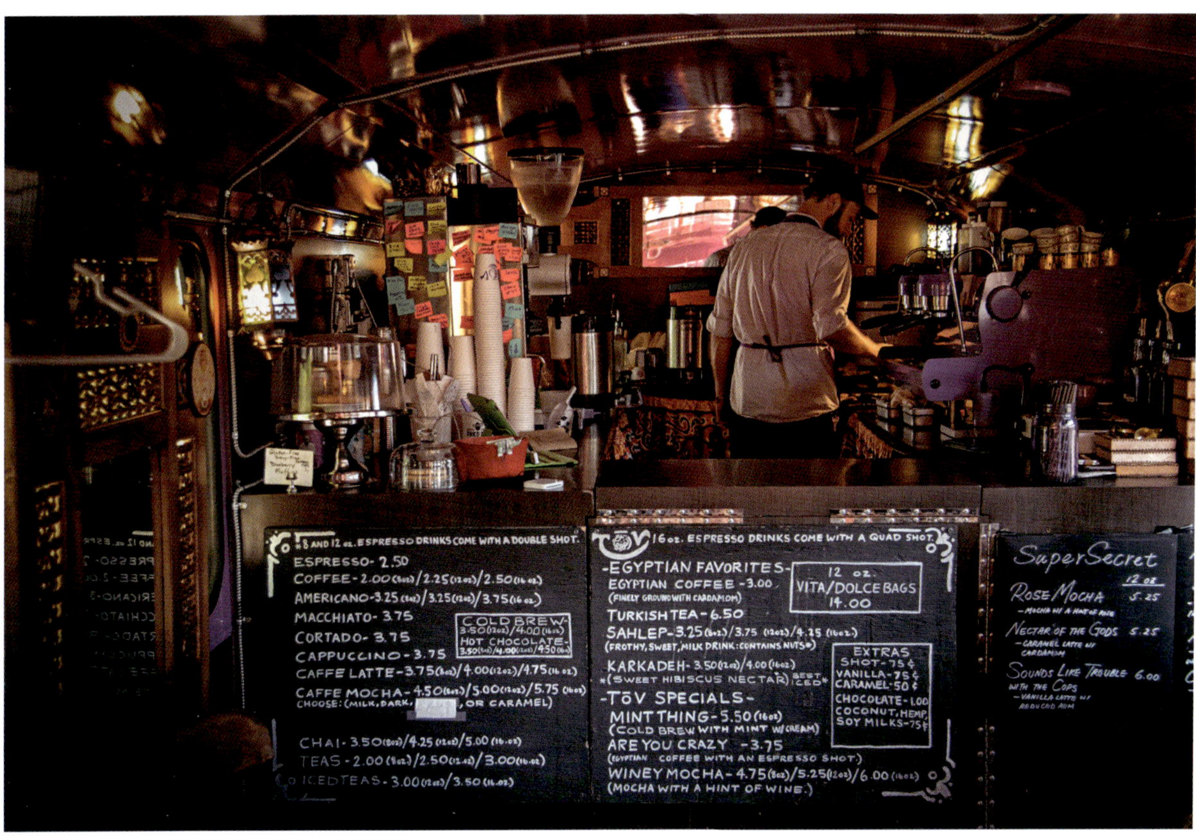


Interior of Tōv Coffee Shop at 32nd & Hawthorne.
*Photo by Barbara Tricarico*

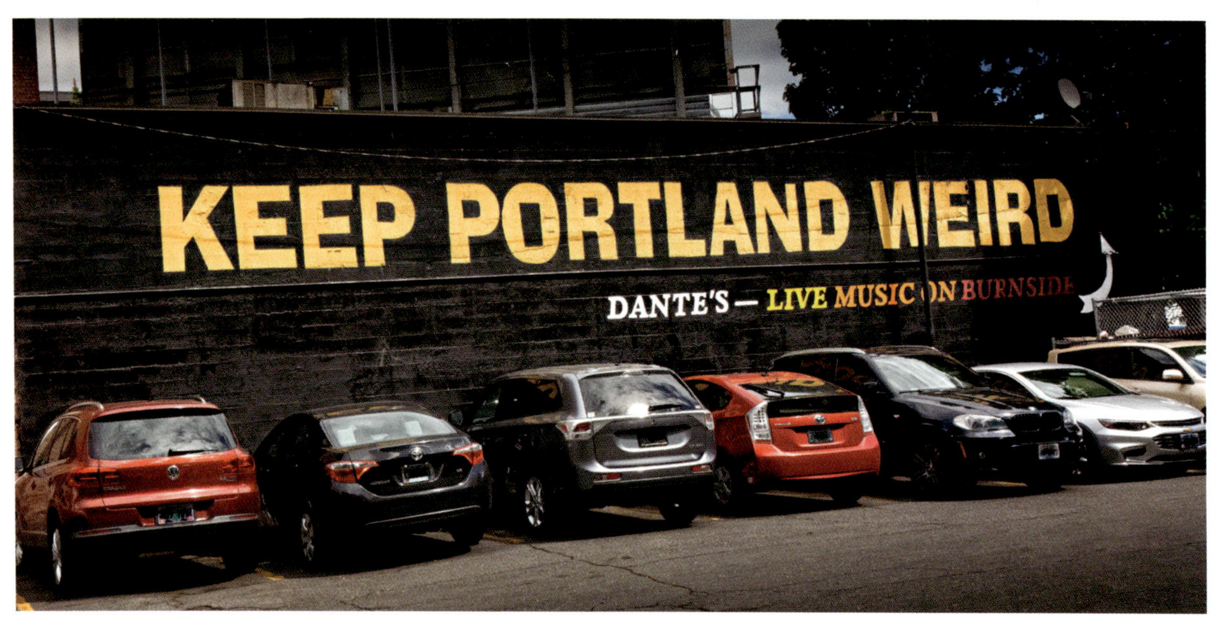


Iconic “Keep Portland Weird” sign. *Photo by Barbara Tricarico*

Portland punk. *Photo by Jay Newman*

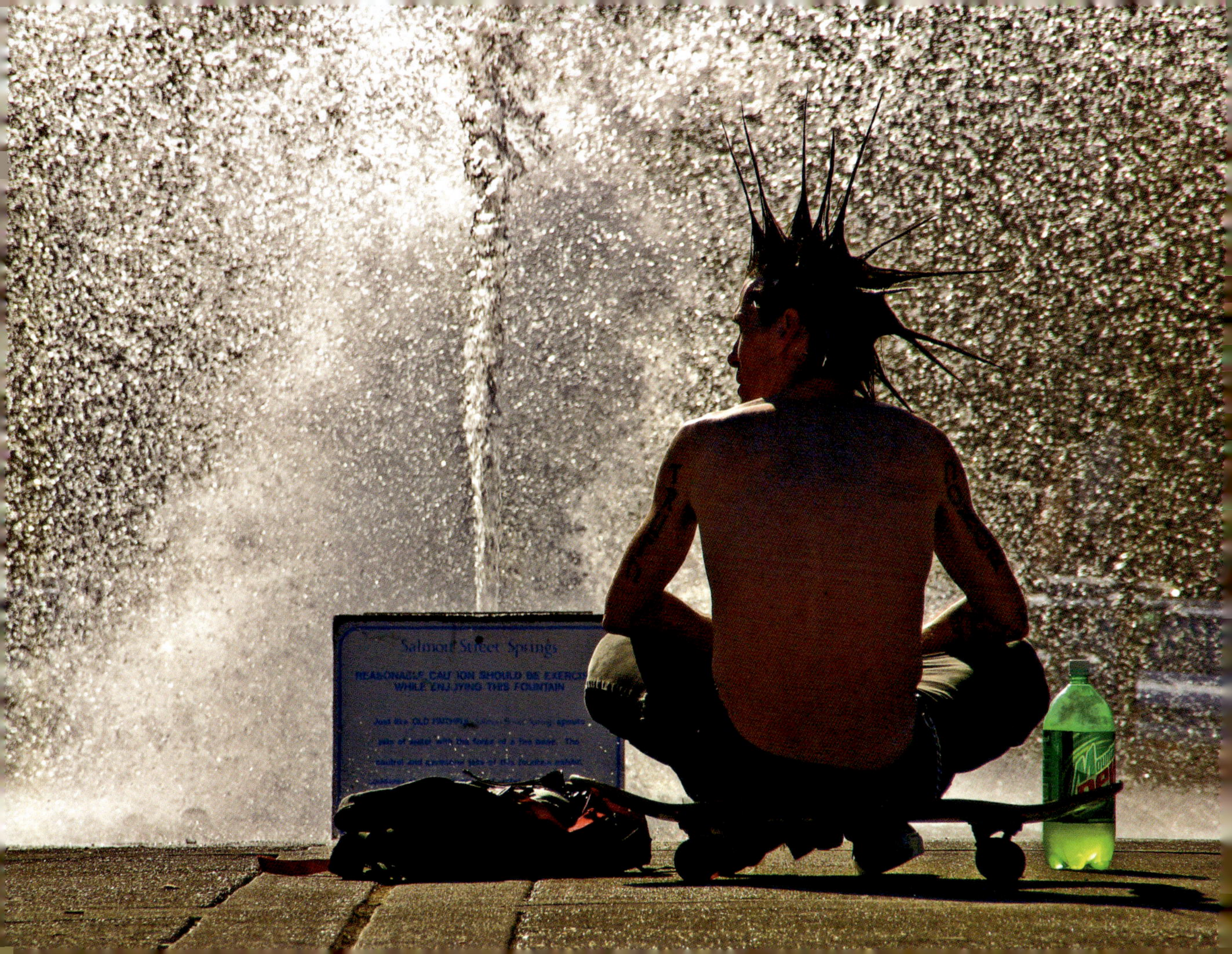
Salmon Street Springs
WHILE ENJOYING THIS FOUNTAIN

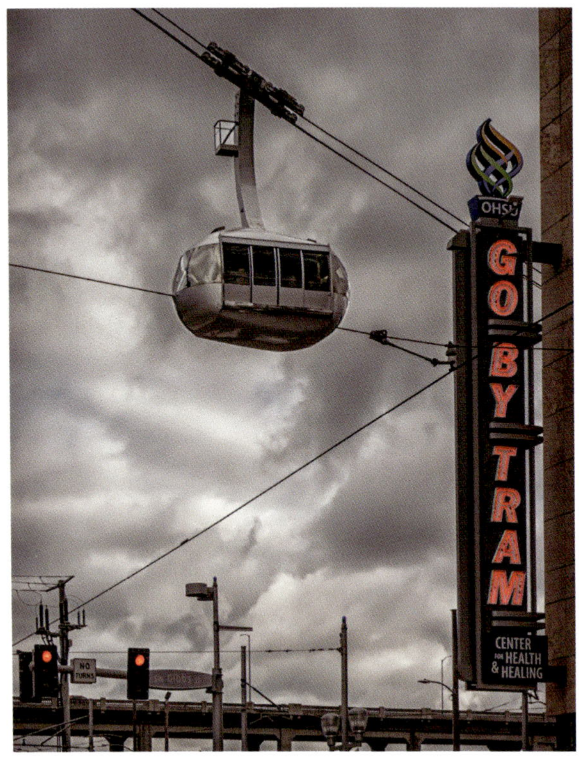


Portland Aerial Tram leaving the South Waterfront district for Oregon Health and Science University (OHSU). *Photo by Barbara Tricarico*

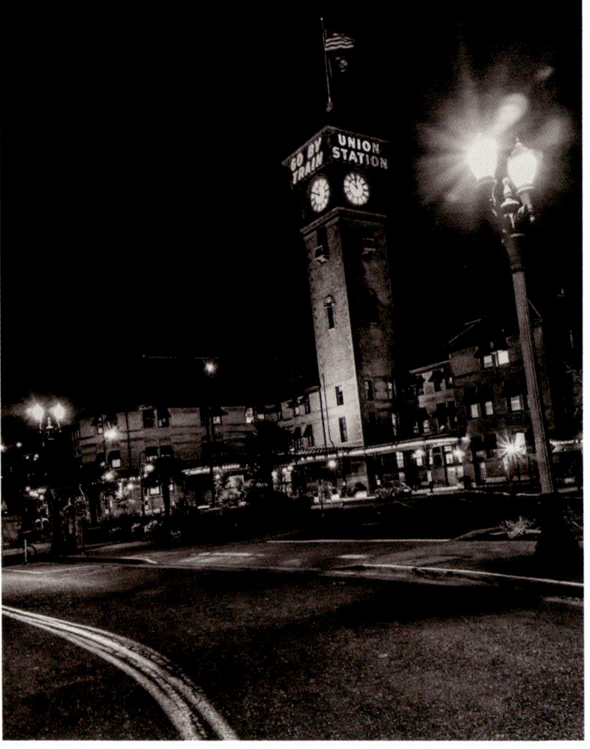


Union Station, built in 1896. The iconic neon "Go by Train" signs were added in 1948. *Photo by Cornelius Matteo*

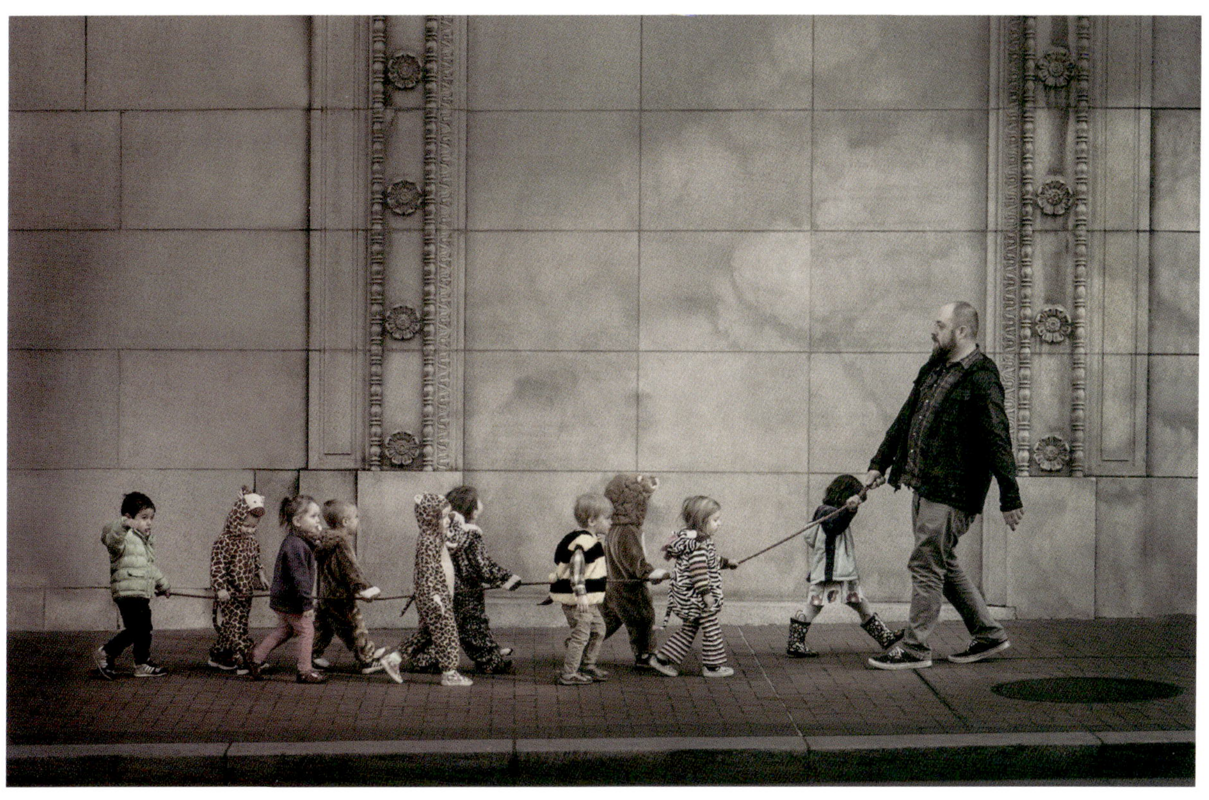

Portland street scene. *Photo by Geri H. Mathewson*

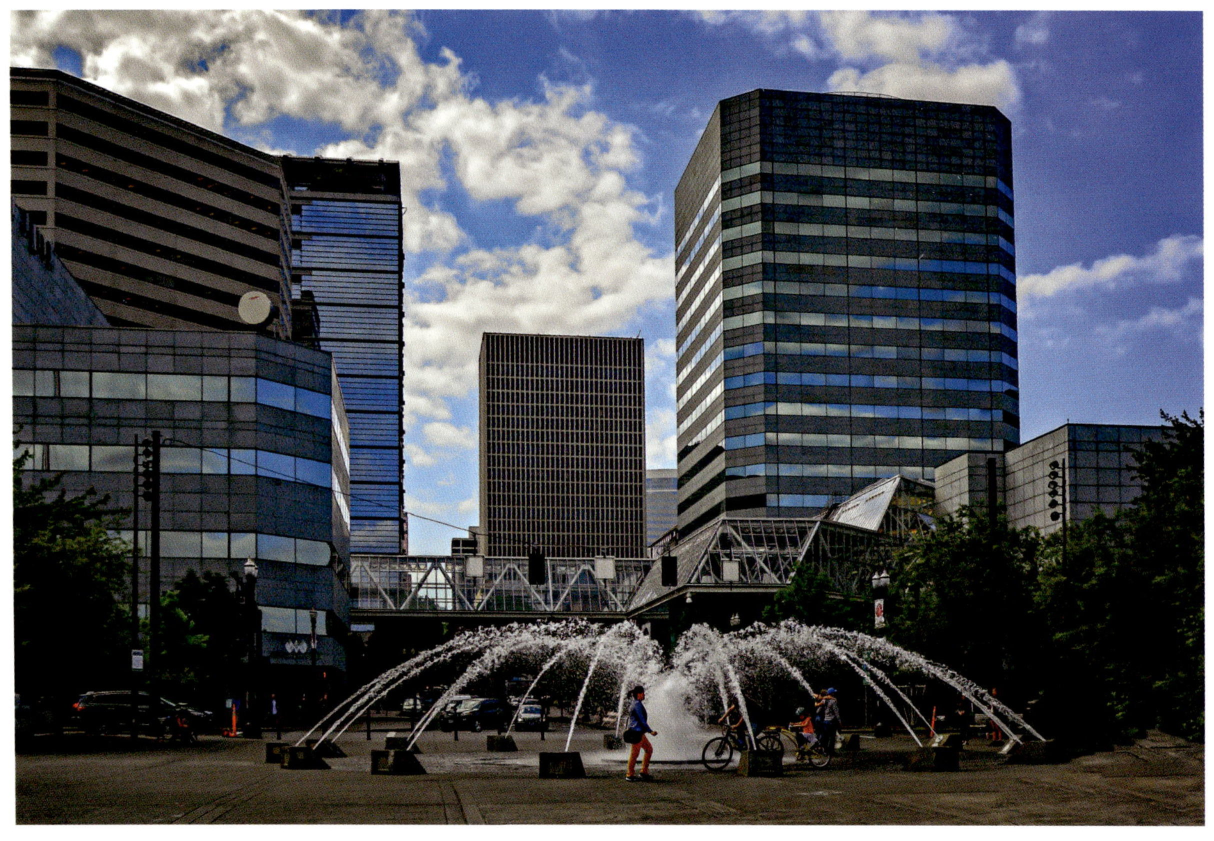

Salmon Street Fountain, Tom McCall Waterfront Park.
*Photo by Tysen Mueller*

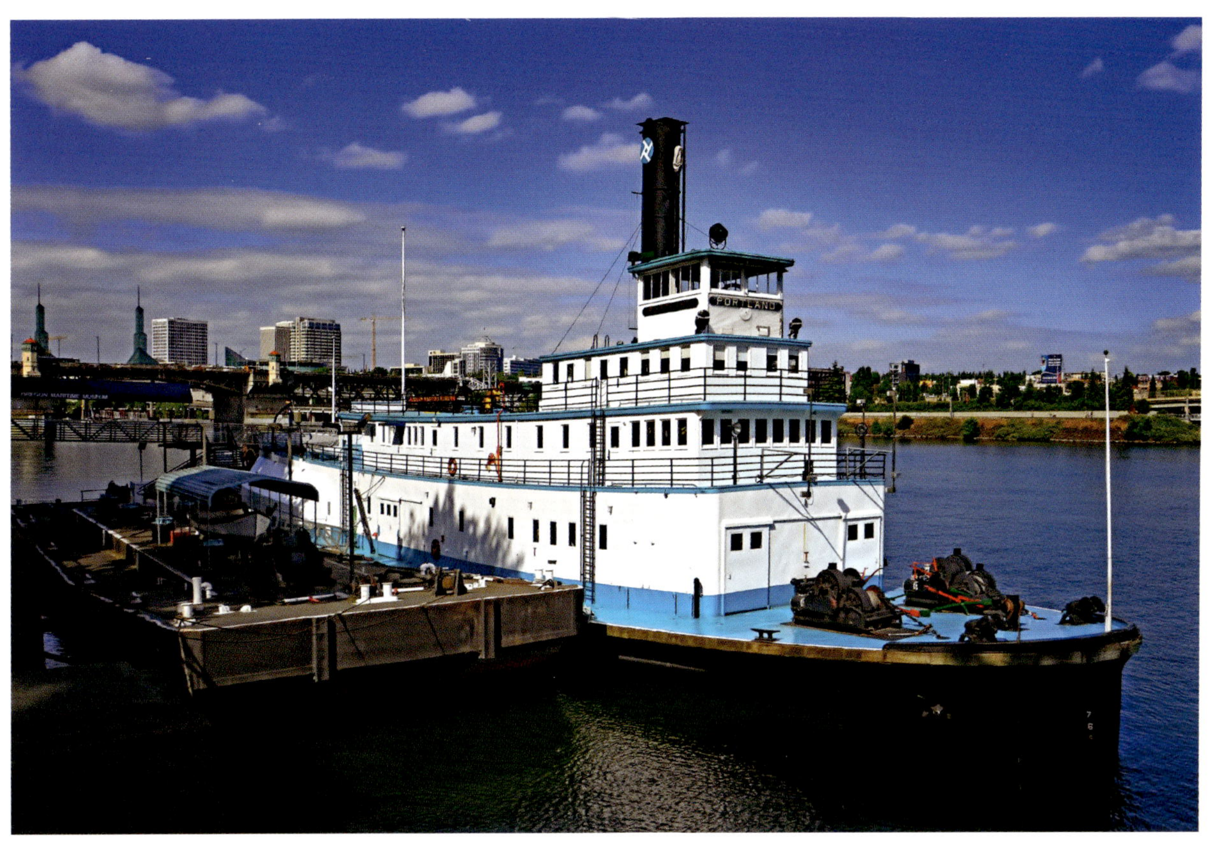


Portland paddle steam tug, built in 1947, on the Willamette River at Tom McCall Waterfront Park. *Photo by Tysen Mueller*

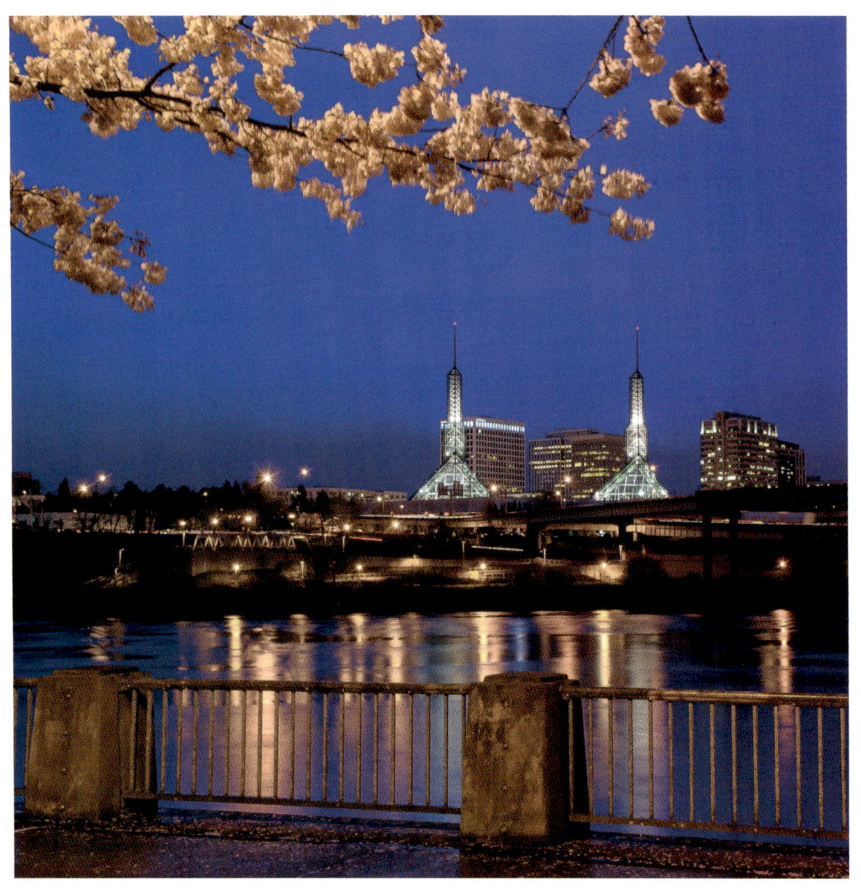

Oregon Convention Center. The iconic twin spire towers provide a distinctive profile on Portland's skyline. *Photo by Clem Paslack*

The Tilikum Crossing Bridge is called Bridge of the People. Opened in 2015, it is the largest car-free bridge in the United States. *Photo by Barbara Tricarico*

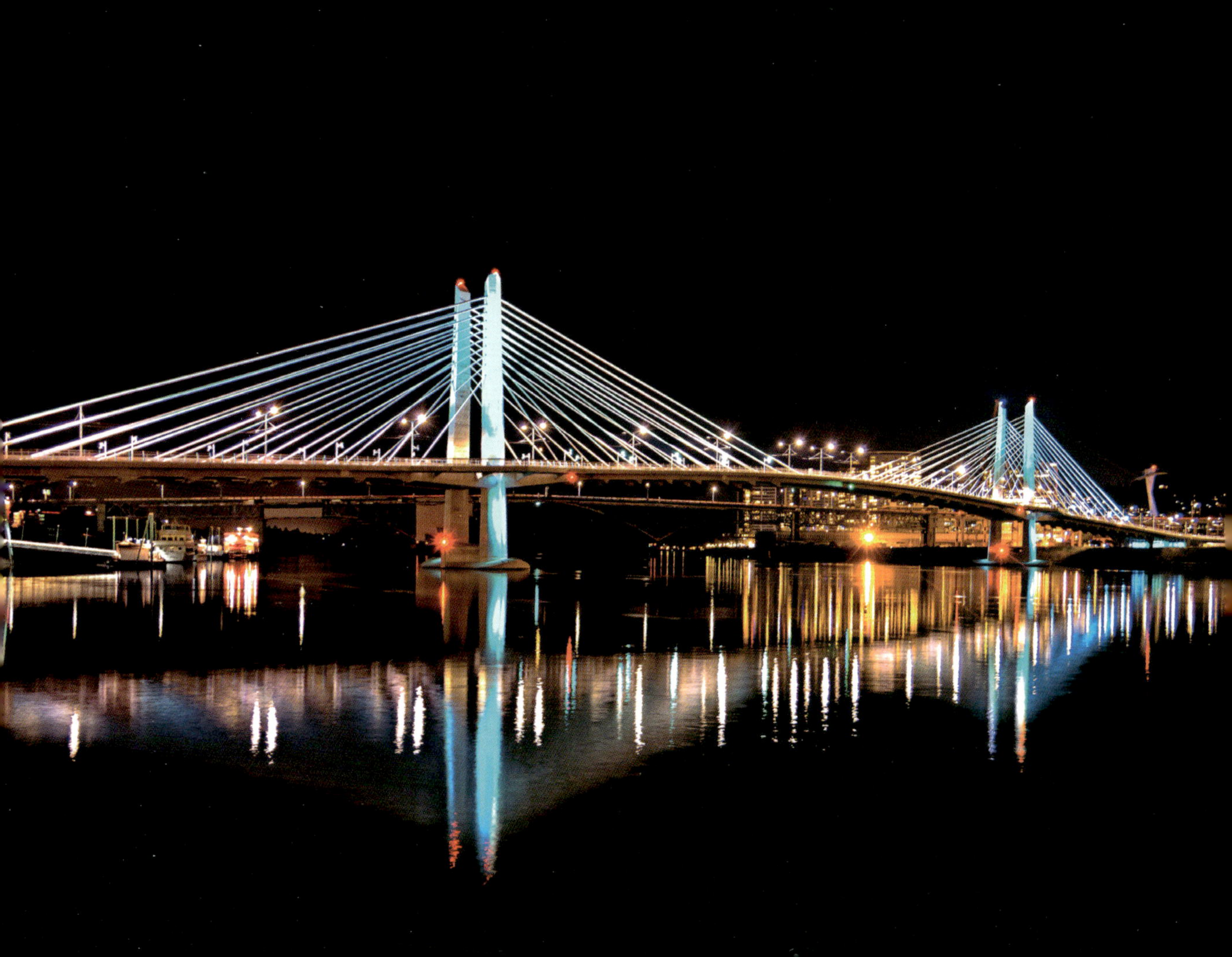

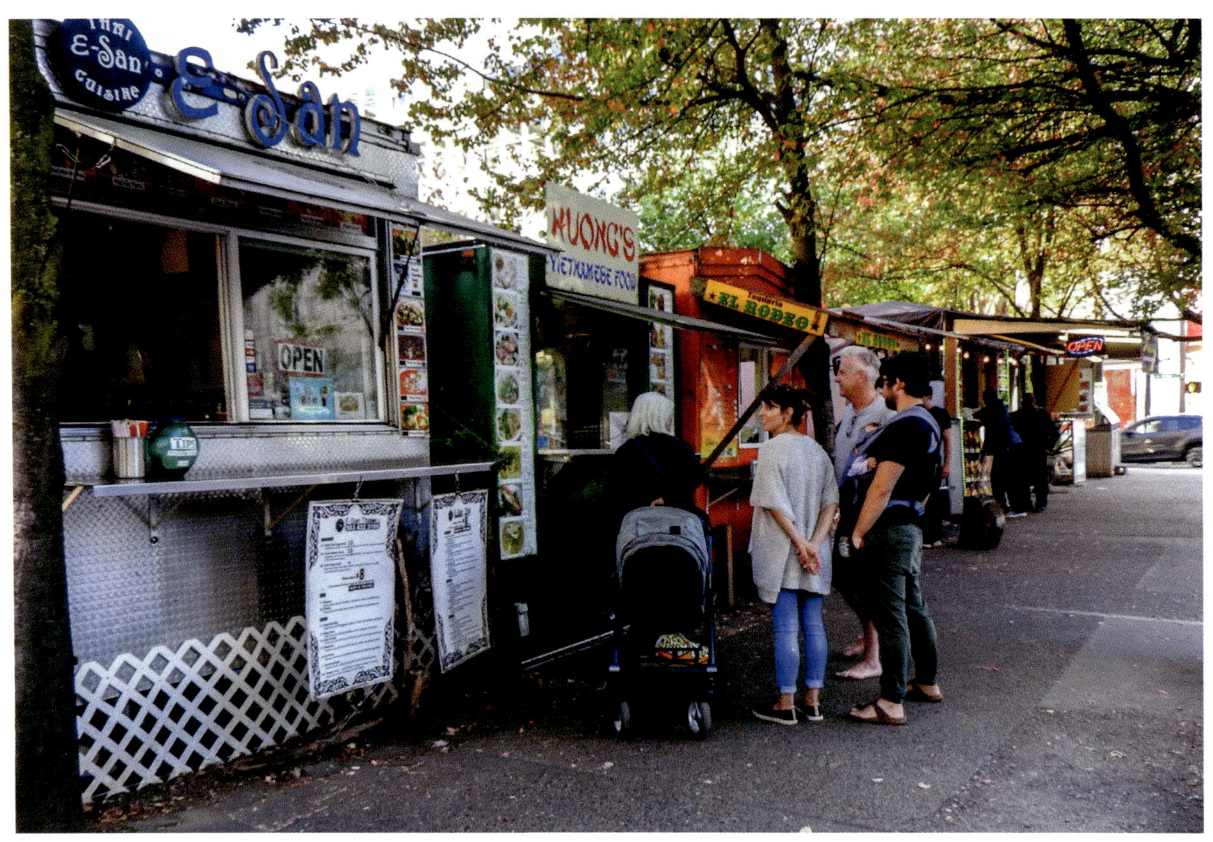


Portland has over 500 food carts grouped in "pods" throughout the city.
*Photo by Charles Hillestad*

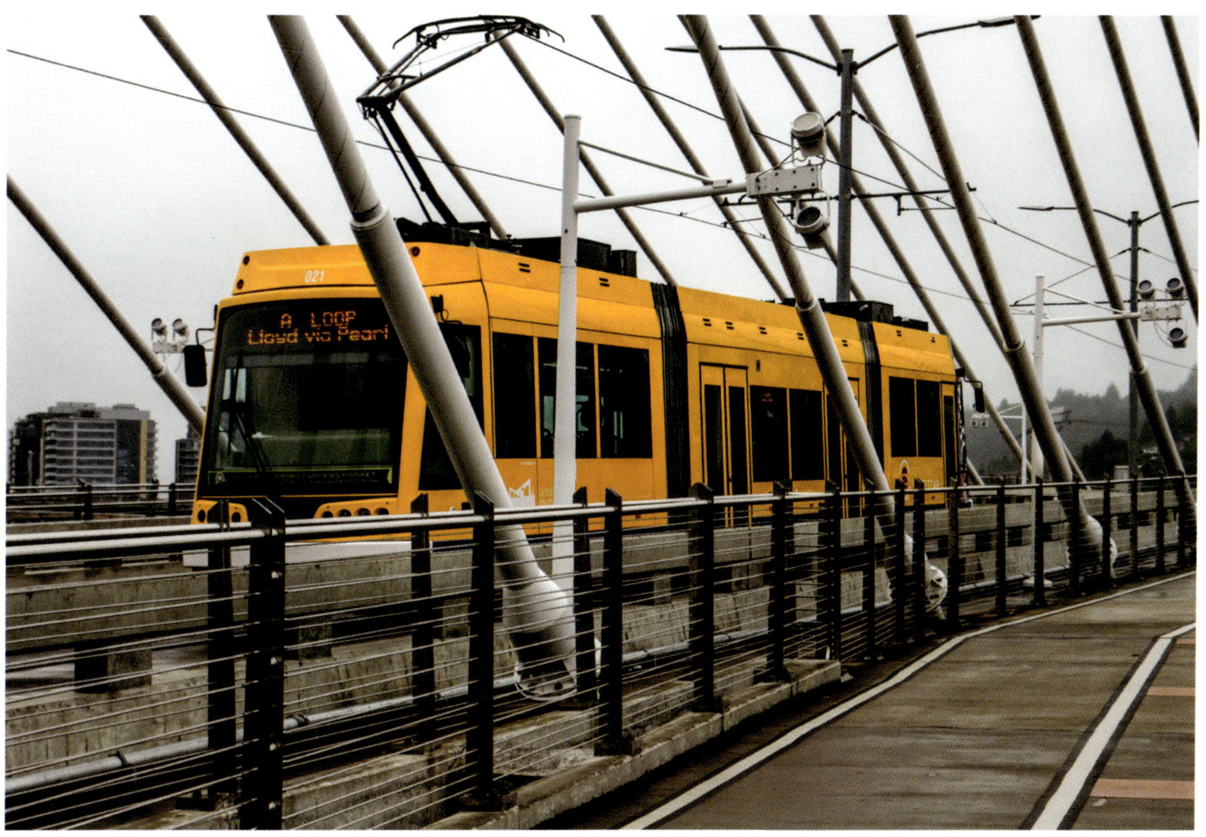


Streetcar on Tilikum Crossing Bridge. *Photo by George F. Peterson*

24

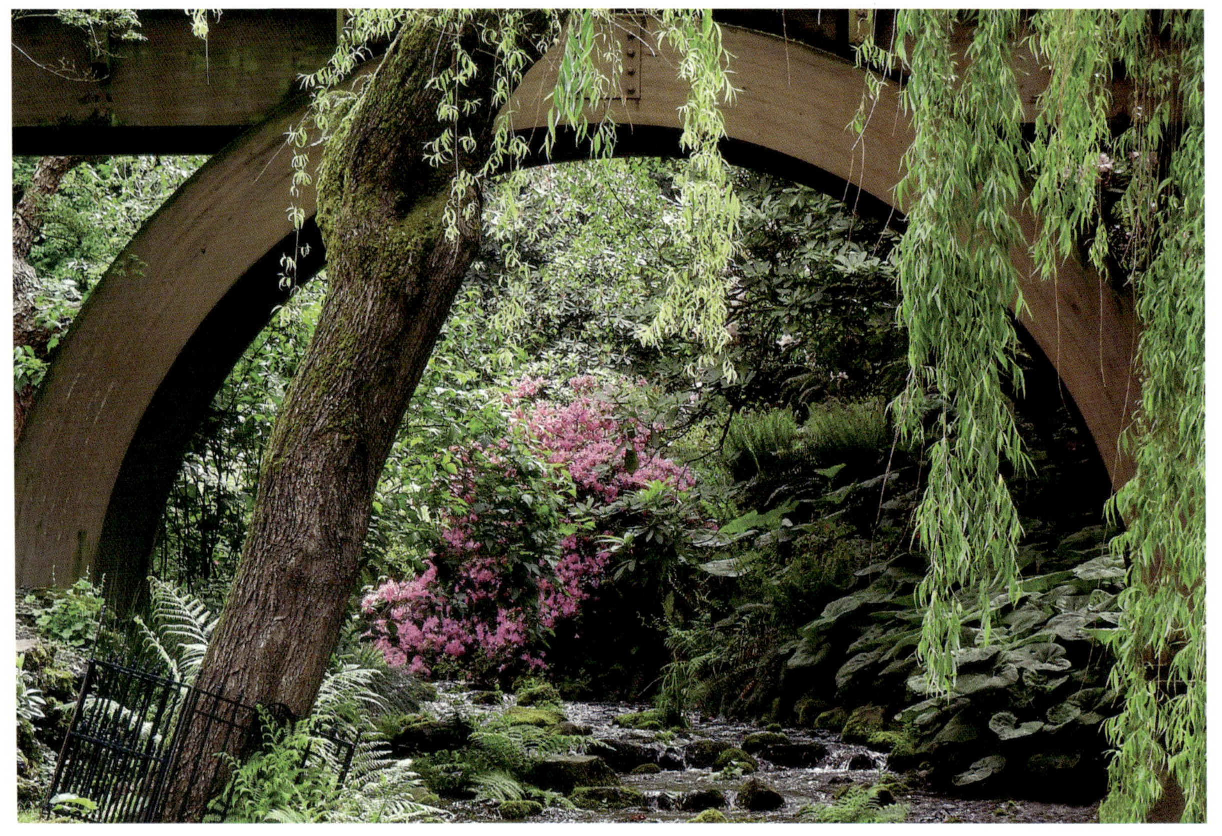

Crystal Springs Rhododendron Garden. *Photo by Charles Hillestad*

Portland Japanese Garden. *Photo by Charles Hillestad*

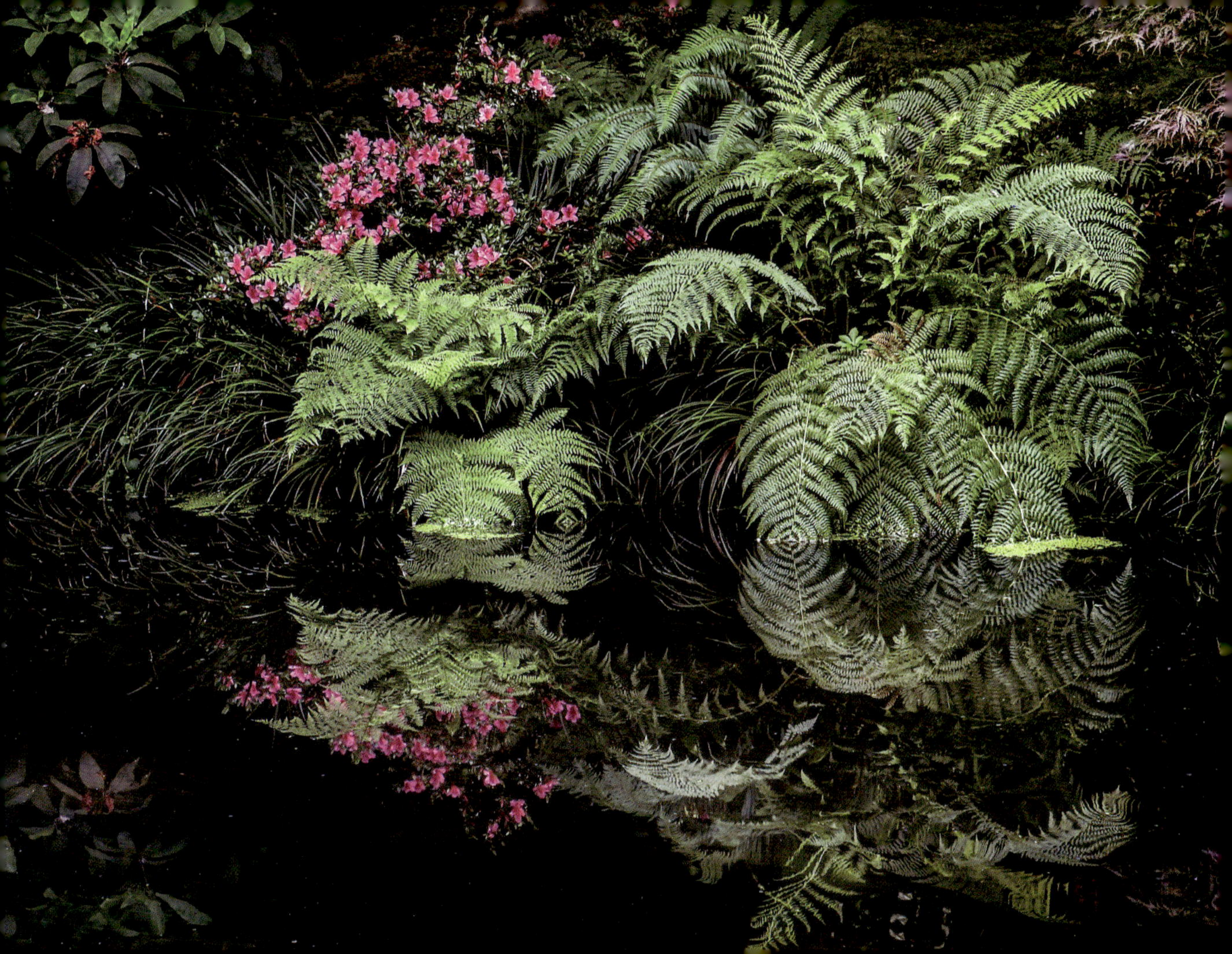

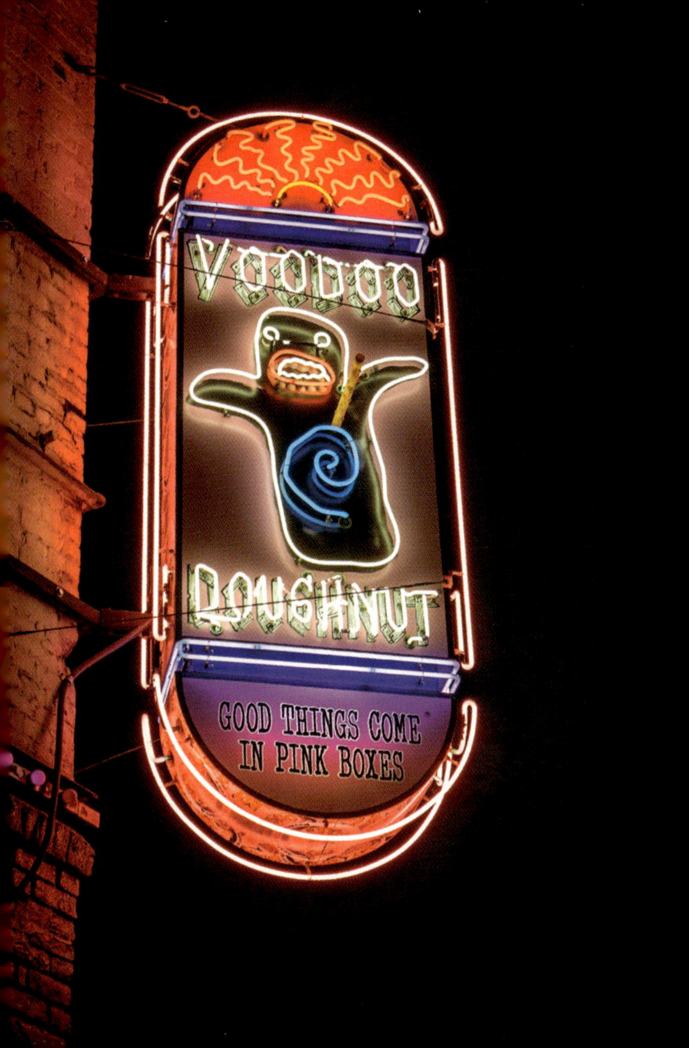


Voodoo Doughnut. The original location, just south of the Burnside Bridge, opened in 2003. *Photo by Barbara Tricarico*

Oregon Convention Center. The twin glass spires provide light into the interior, which houses the world's largest Foucault Pendulum. *Photo by Barbara Tricarico*

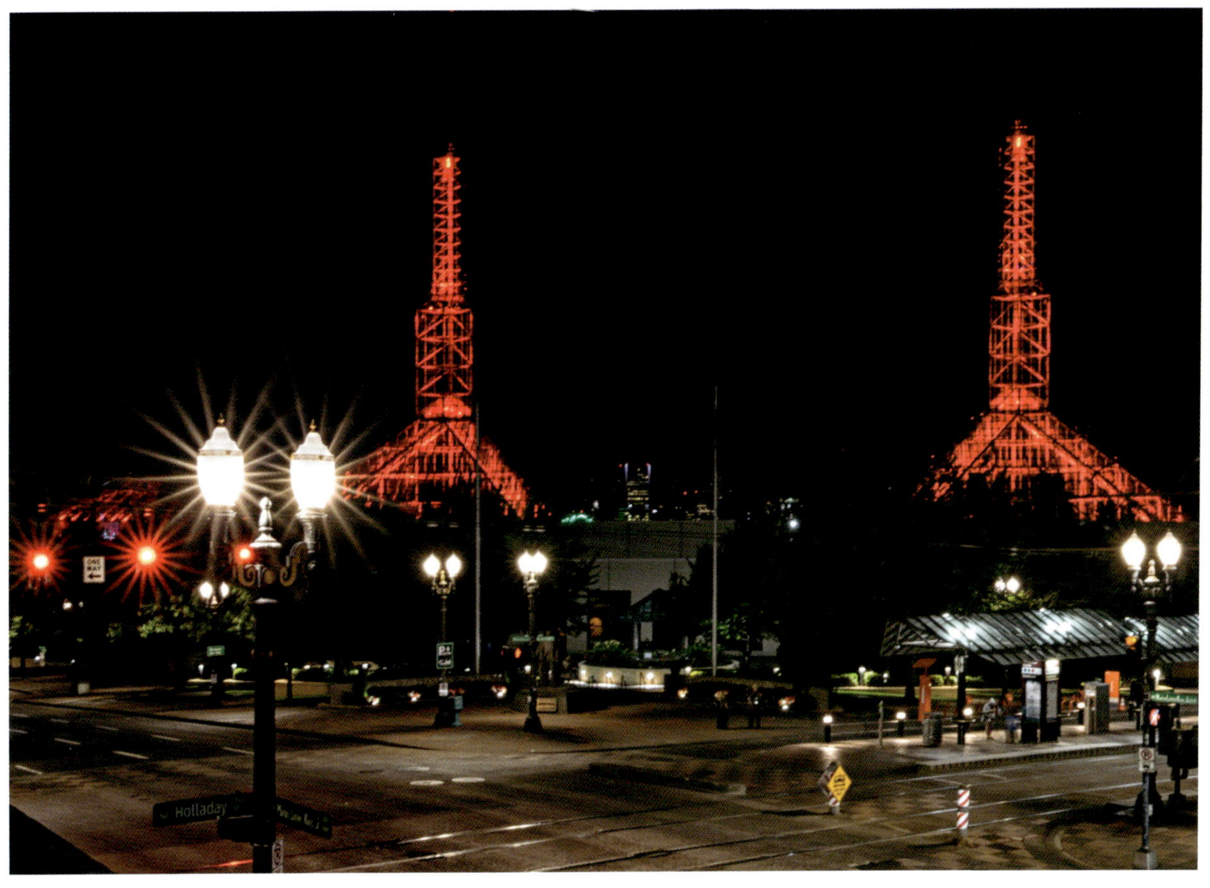
Holladay

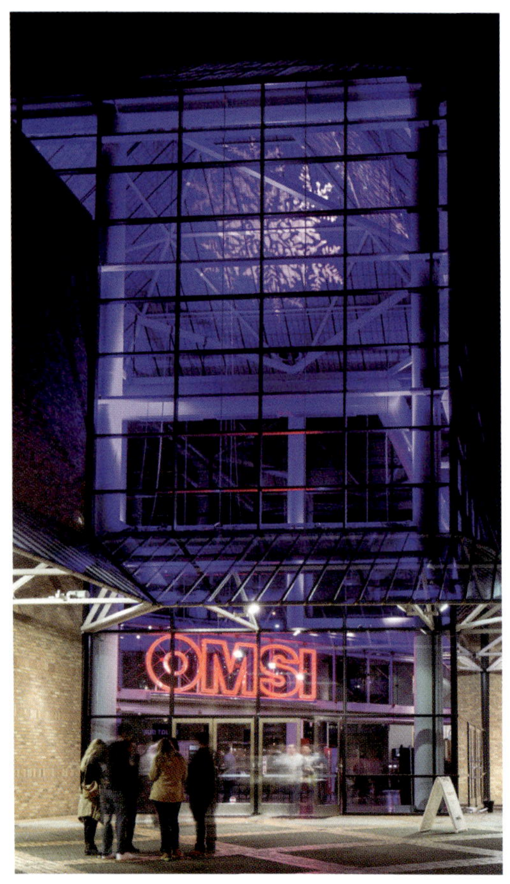


Oregon Museum of Science and Industry (OMSI). *Photo by Barbara Tricarico*

Tilikum Crossing Bridge. *Photo by Barbara Tricarico*

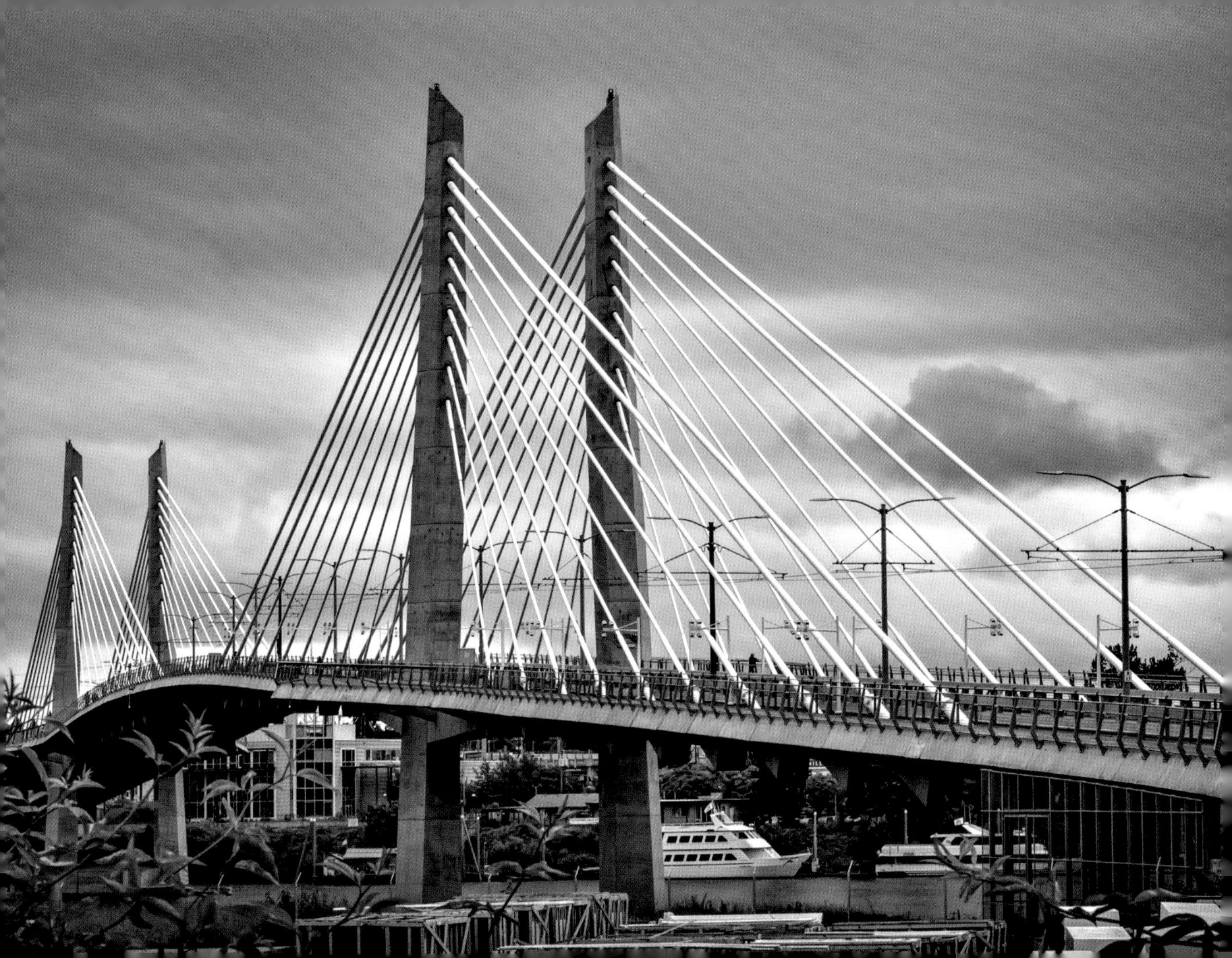

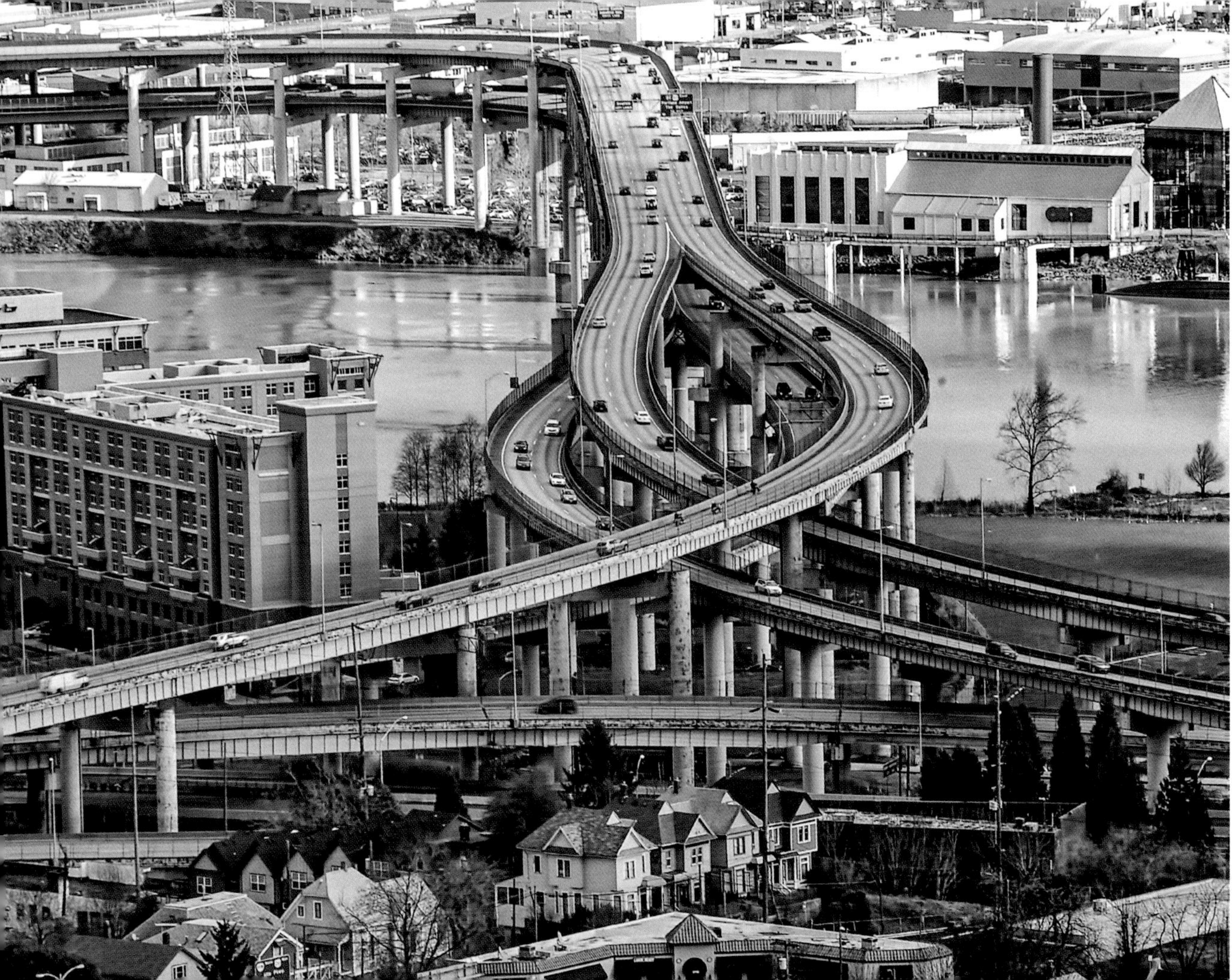

Marquam Bridge and Willamette River from Portland Aerial Tram. *Photo by Barbara Tricarico*

The Interstate Bridge crosses the Columbia River between Vancouver and Portland on Interstate 5. It opened in 1917. *Photo by Charles Hillestad*

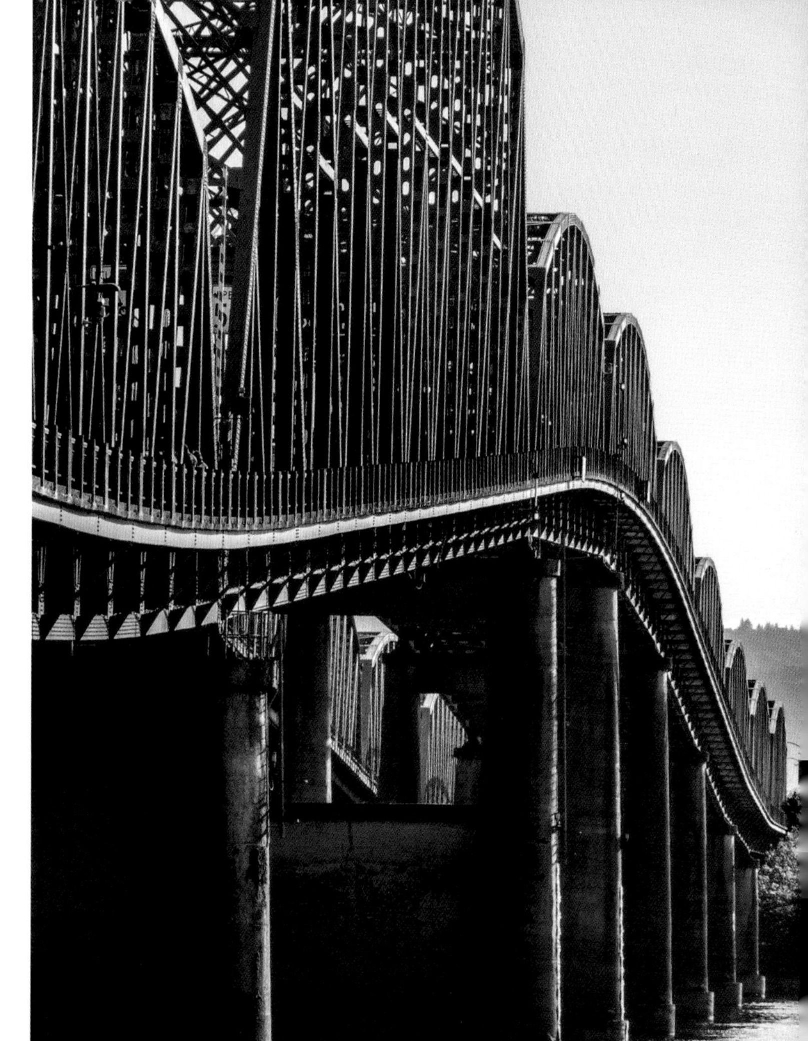

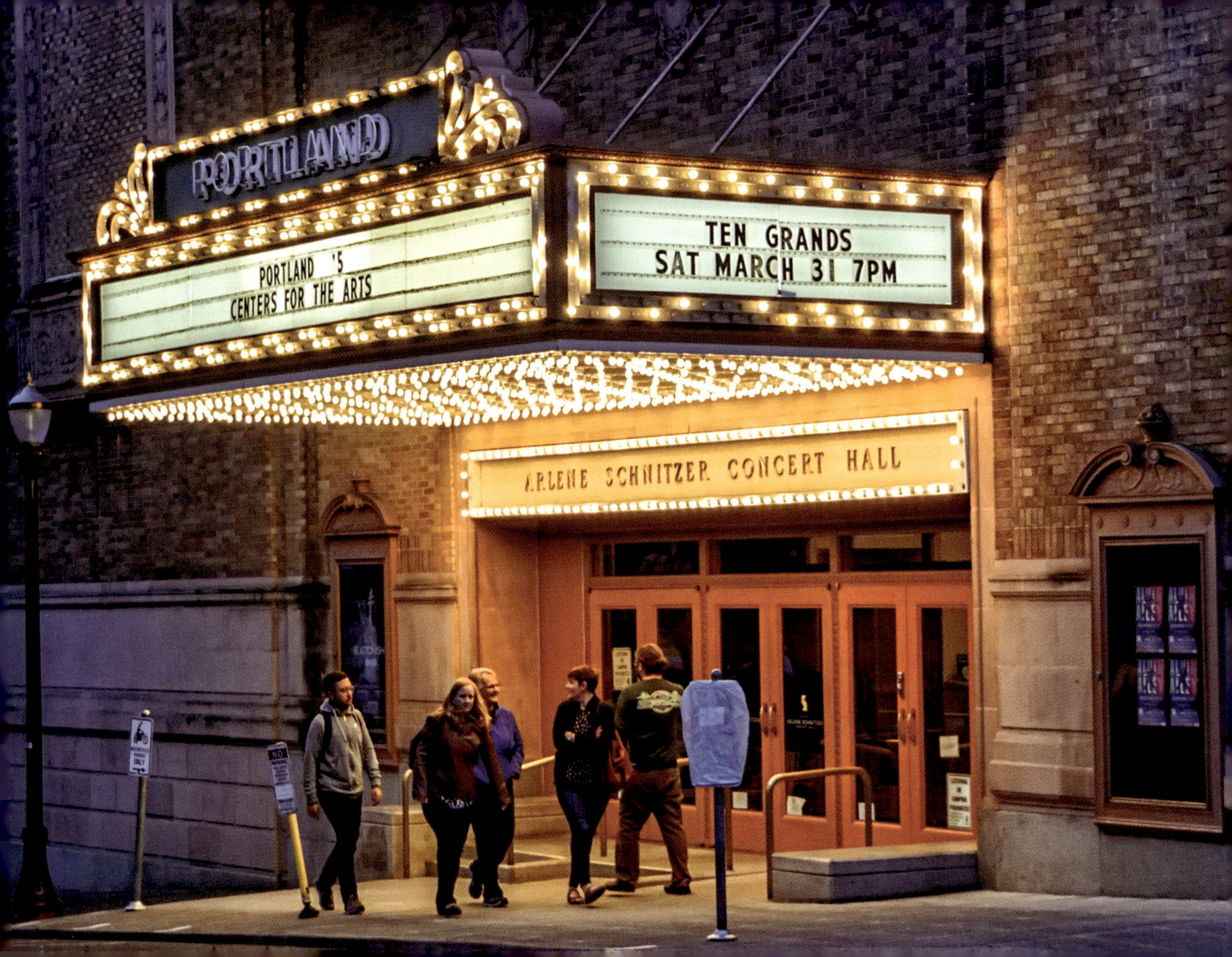
PORTLAND
PORTLAND '5
CENTERS FOR THE ARTS
TEN GRANDS
SAT MARCH 31 7PM
ARLENE SCHNITZER CONCERT HALL

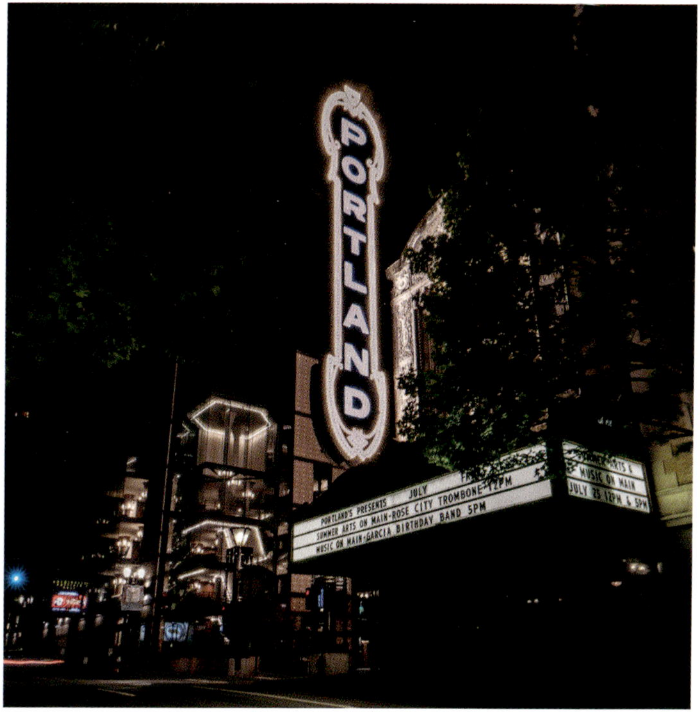

Arlene Schnitzer Concert Hall, affectionately called "The Schnitz" by locals. *Photo by Neal R. Thompson*

Historic "Portland" sign at Arlene Schnitzer Concert Hall. *Photo by Barbara Tricarico*

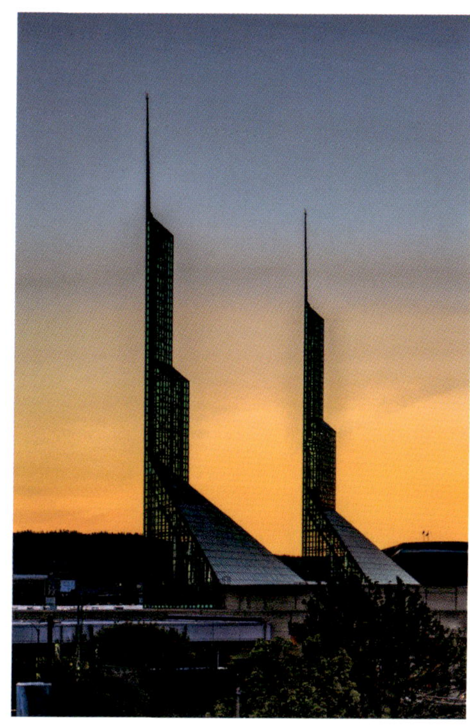

Twin spires, Oregon Convention Center, at sunset. *Photo by Barbara Tricarico*

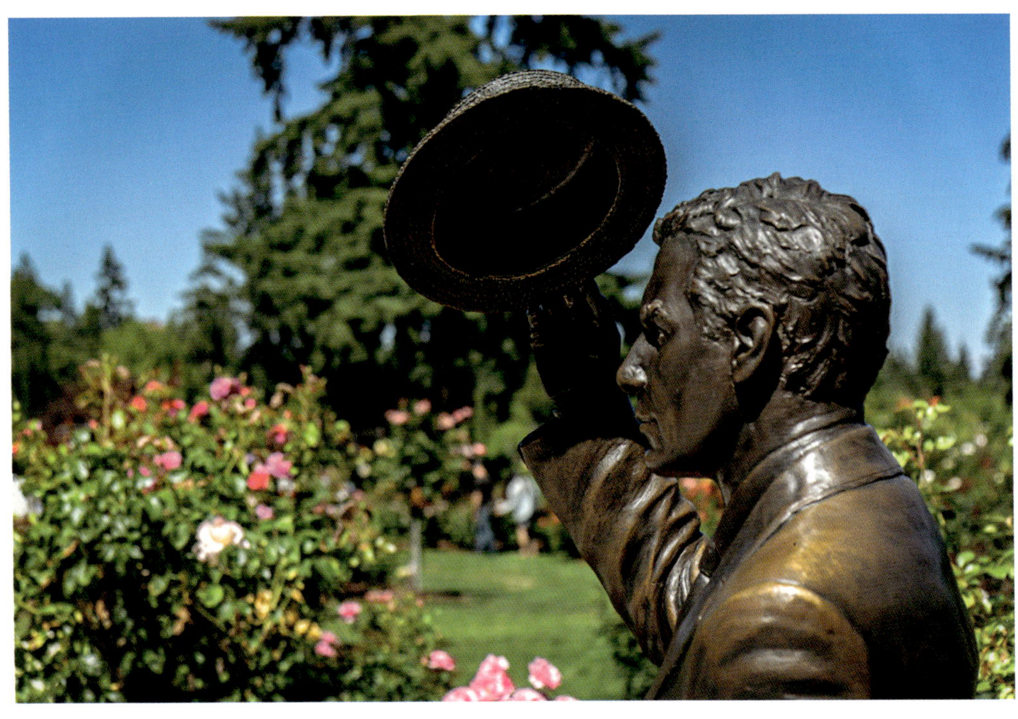

*Royal Rosarian* is a 2011 bronze sculpture by Bill Bane in the International Rose Test Garden, Washington Park. *Photo by Barbara Tricarico*

Portland is known as the City of Roses. *Photo by Alana Lynn Starkweather*

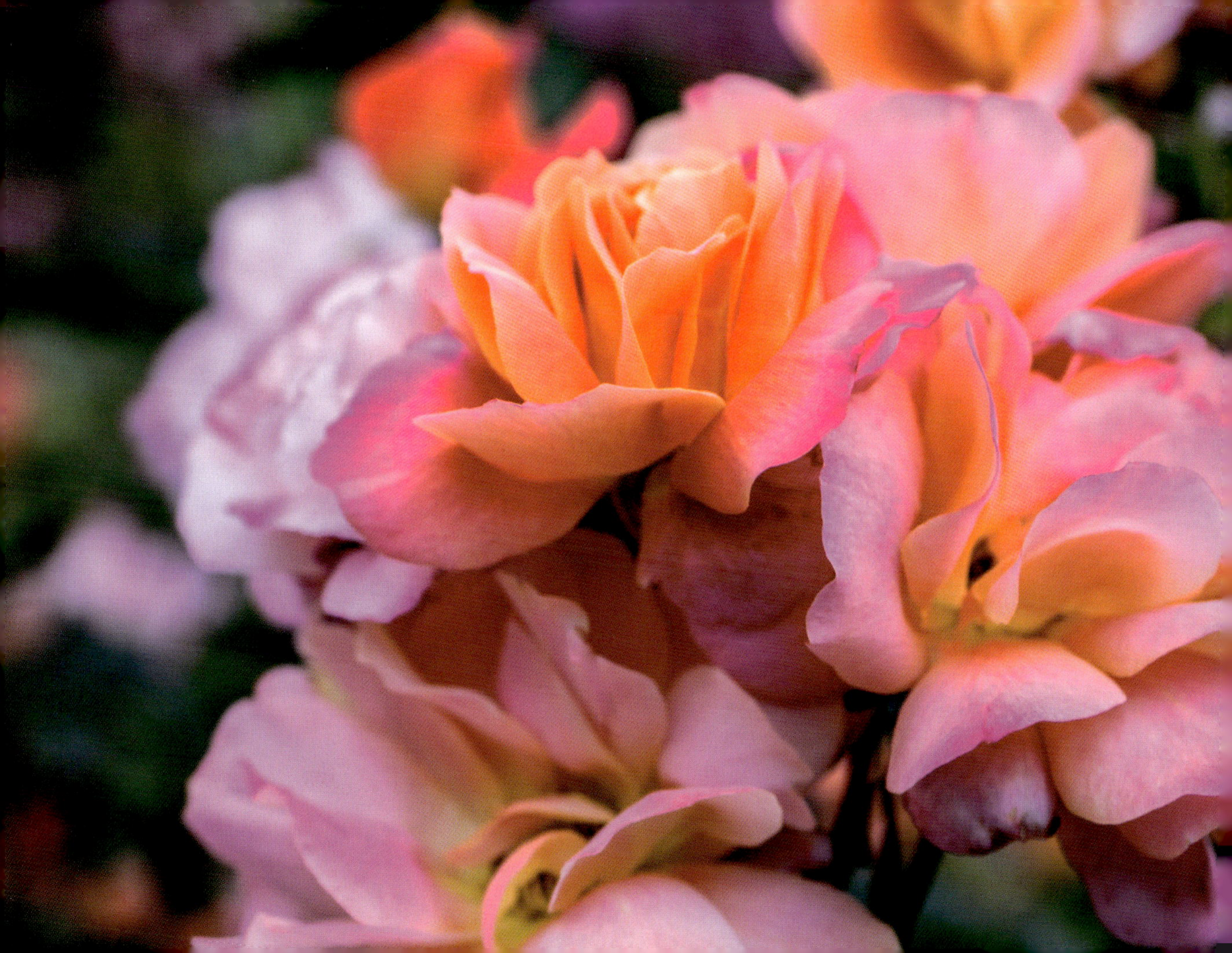

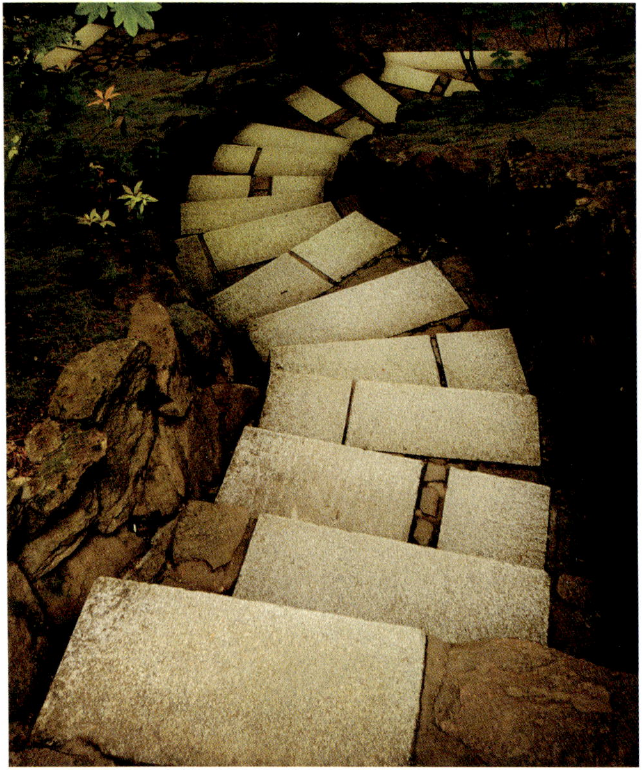

Portland Japanese Garden steps in Washington Park. *Photo by John Kirk*

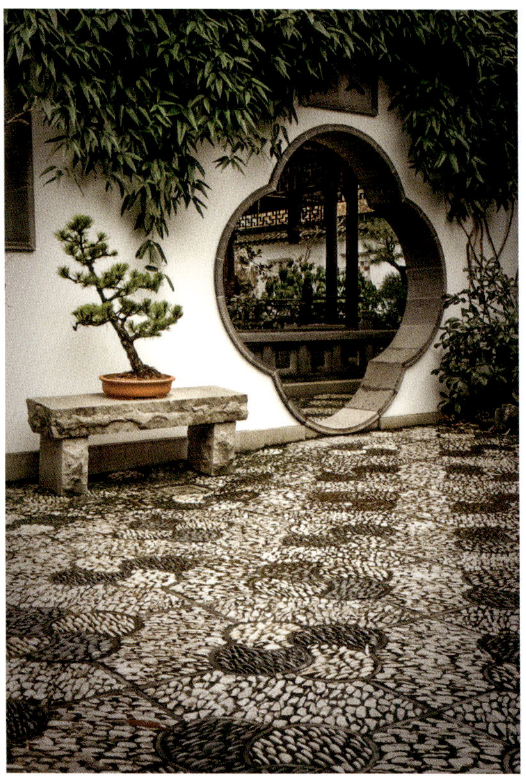

Lan Su Chinese Garden is a walled garden in Old Town Chinatown. *Photo by Kate Geary*

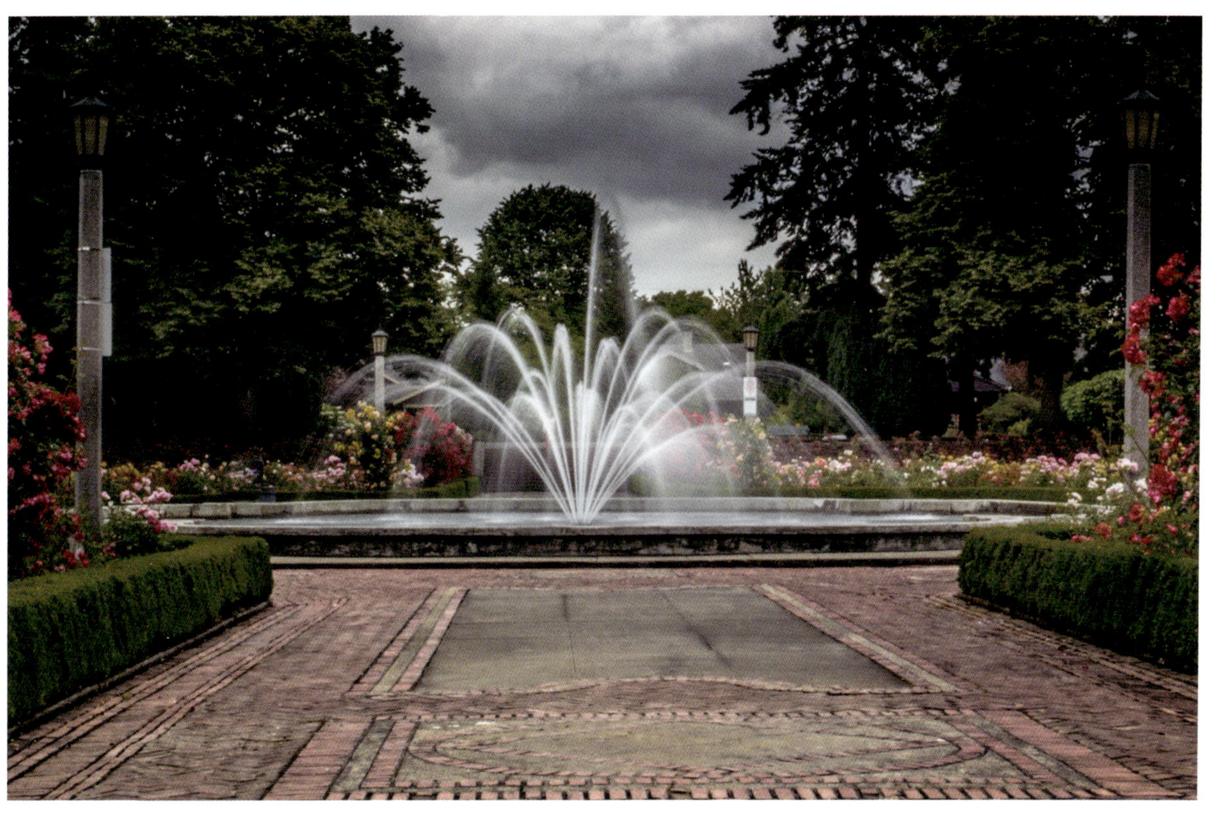

Rose City Park. *Photo by Alana Lynn Starkweather*

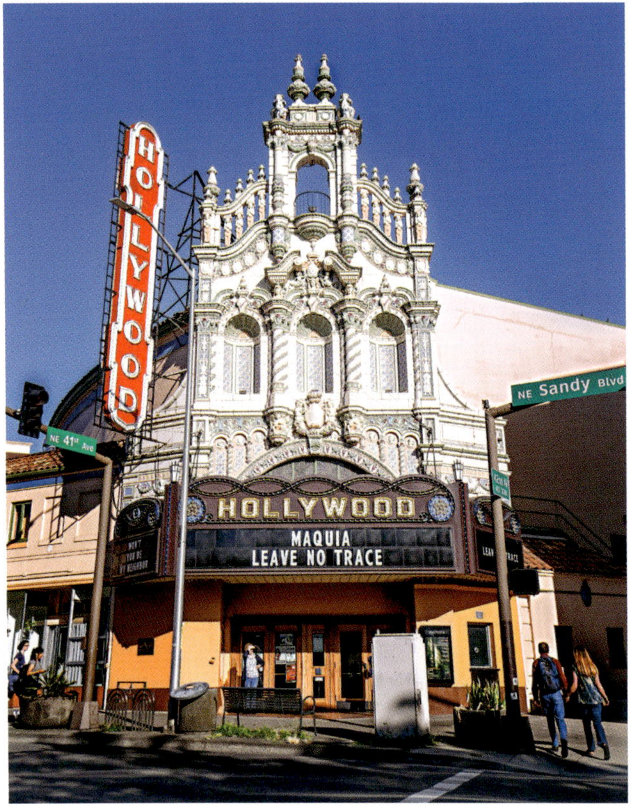

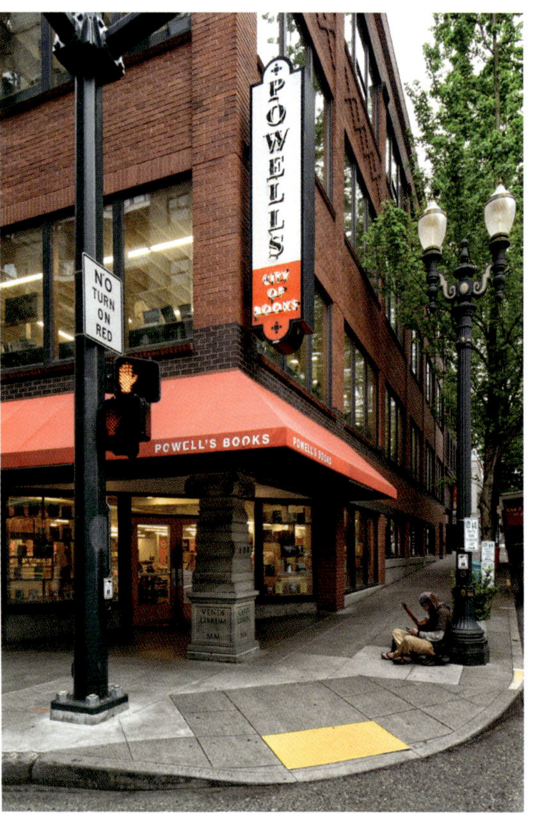


The Hollywood Theatre opened in 1926. *Photo by Cornelius Matteo*

Powell's Books, the world's largest independent bookstore. *Photo by Barbara Tricarico*

Pioneer Square, often called "Portland's Living Room," and Pioneer Courthouse. *Photo by Tysen Mueller*

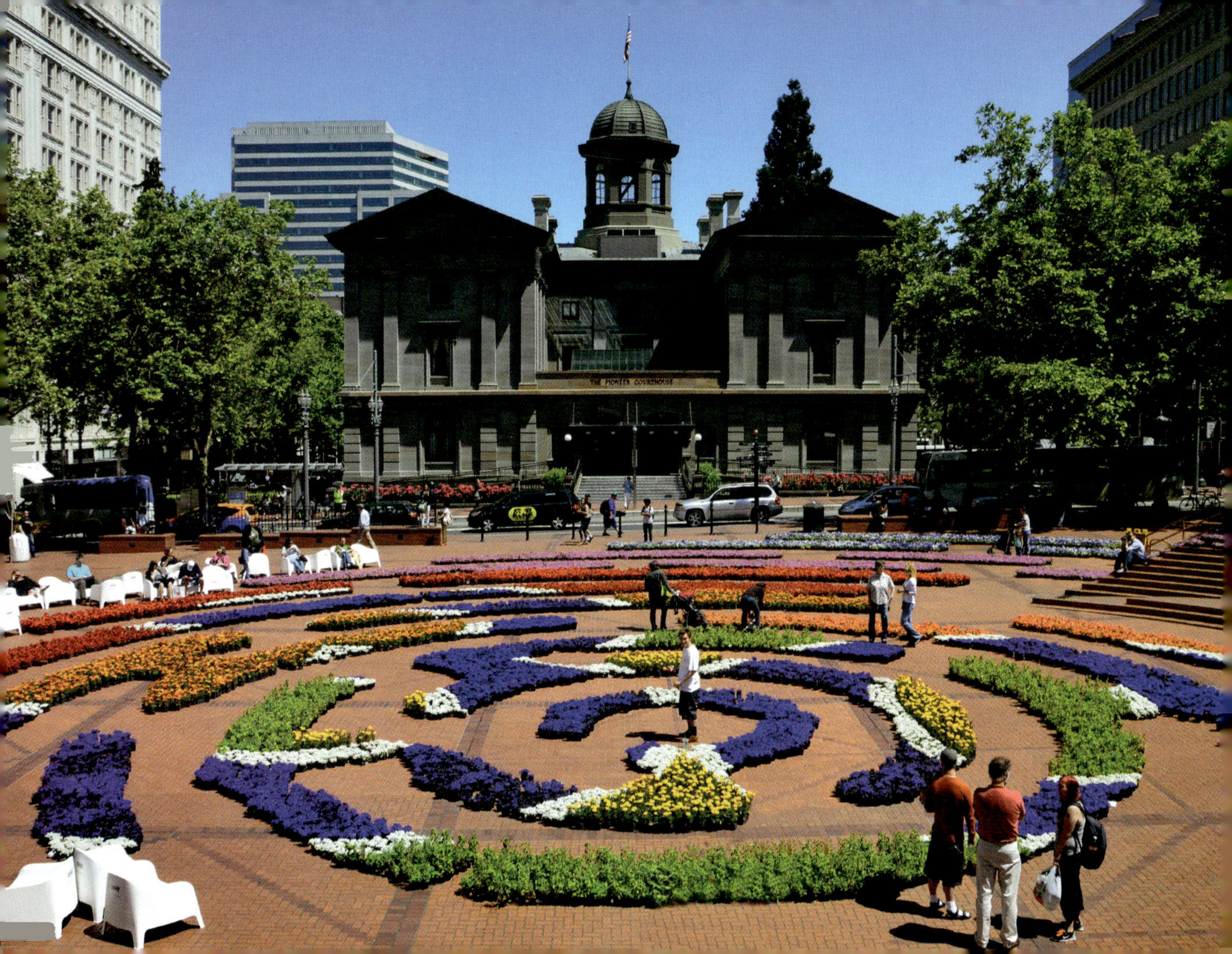
THE PIONEER COURTHOUSE

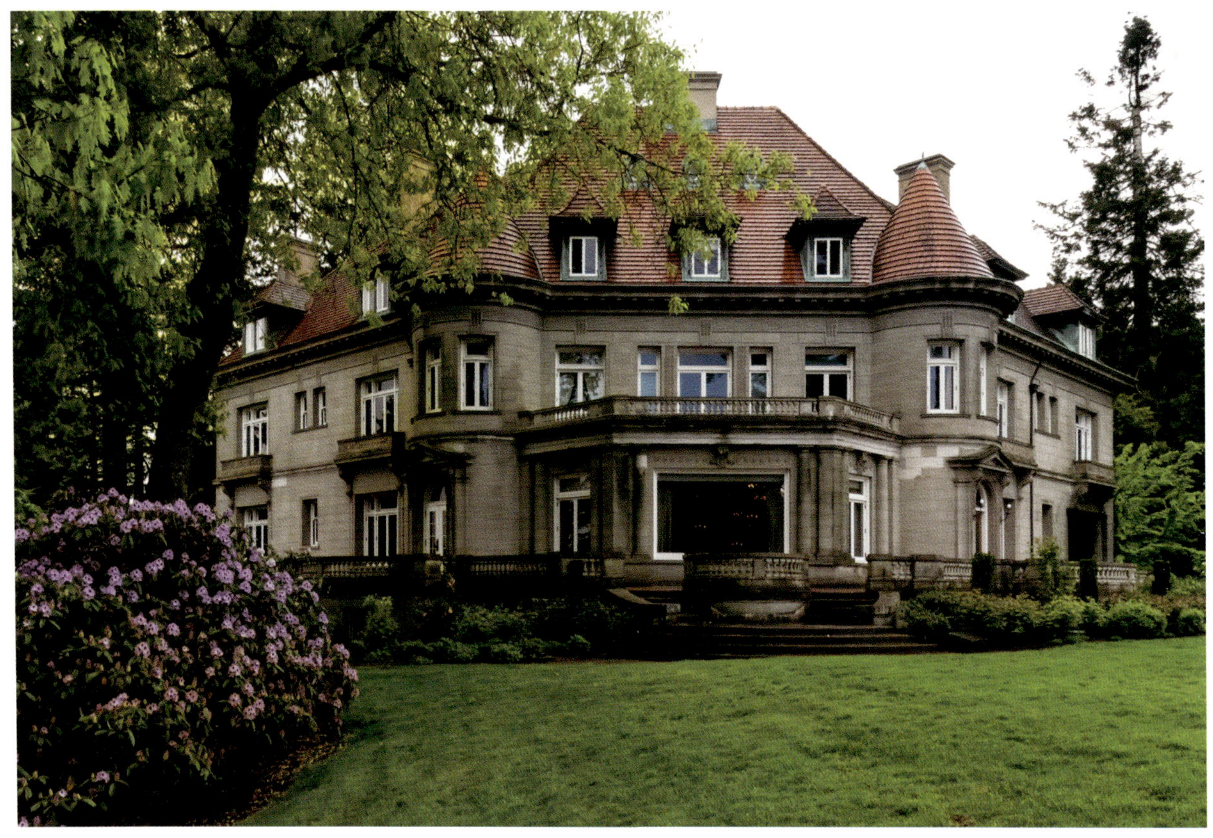

Pittock Mansion, built in 1914 by *Oregonian* publisher Henry Pittock and his wife, Georgiana. Both traveled on the Oregon Trail from the East in 1853 and 1854, respectively. *Photo by Barbara Tricarico*

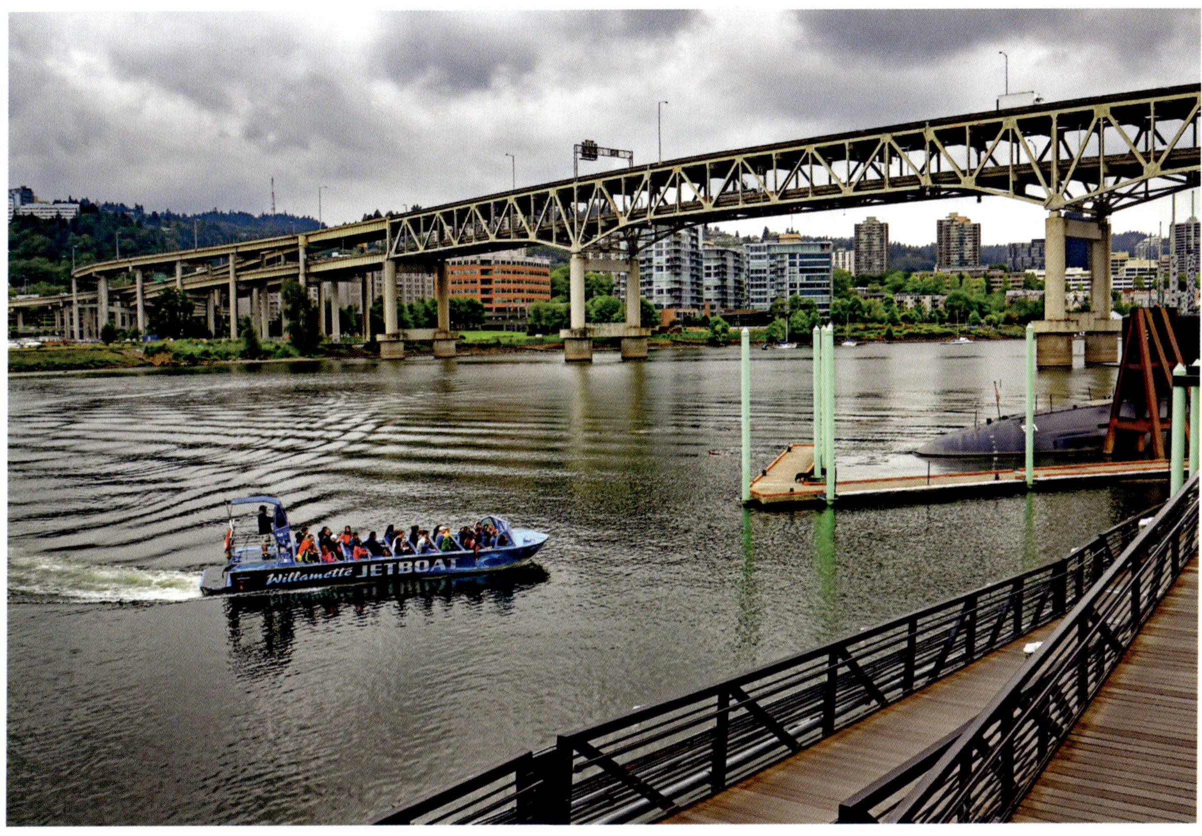




Willamette Jetboat and Marquam Bridge from Oregon Museum of Science and Industry (OMSI). *Photo by Tysen Mueller*

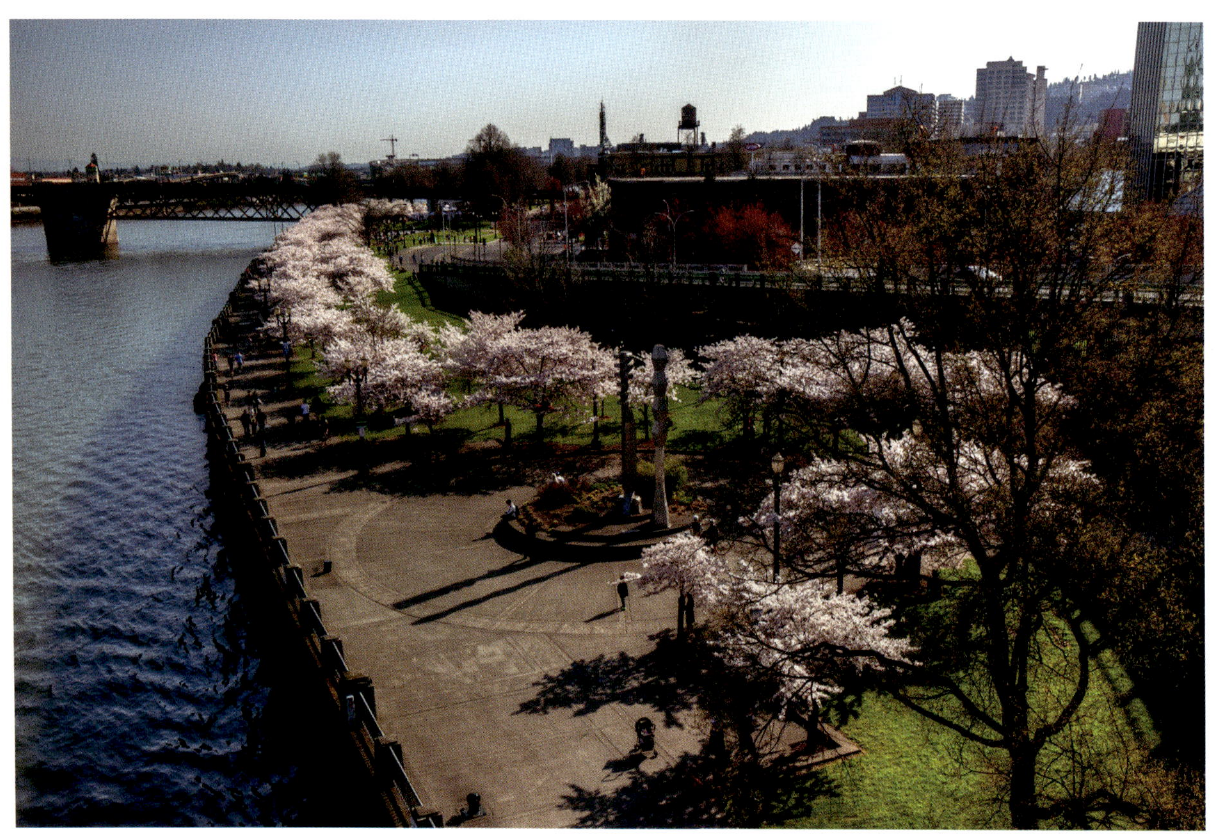

Portland waterfront and cherry blossoms at Tom McCall Park. *Photo by Sue Newman*

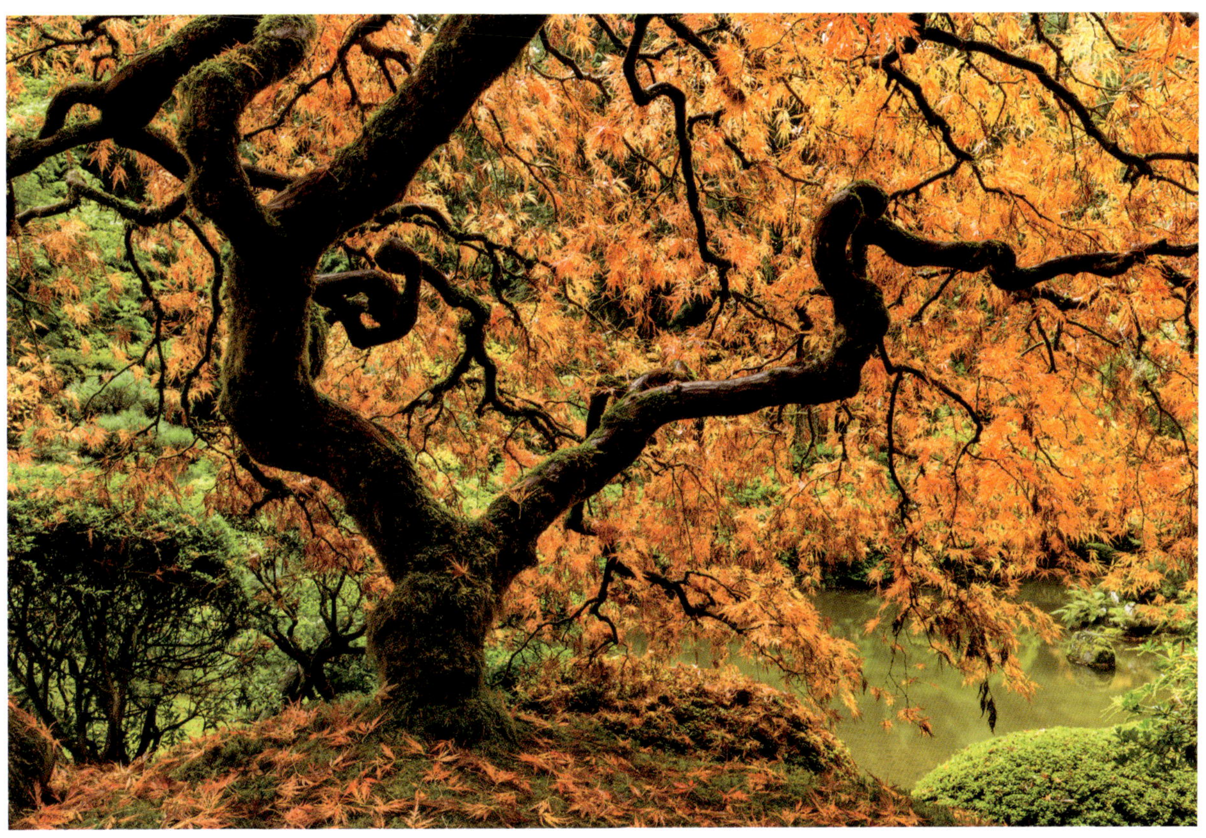



Japanese maple tree, Portland Japanese Garden.
*Photo by Vldn Taylor*

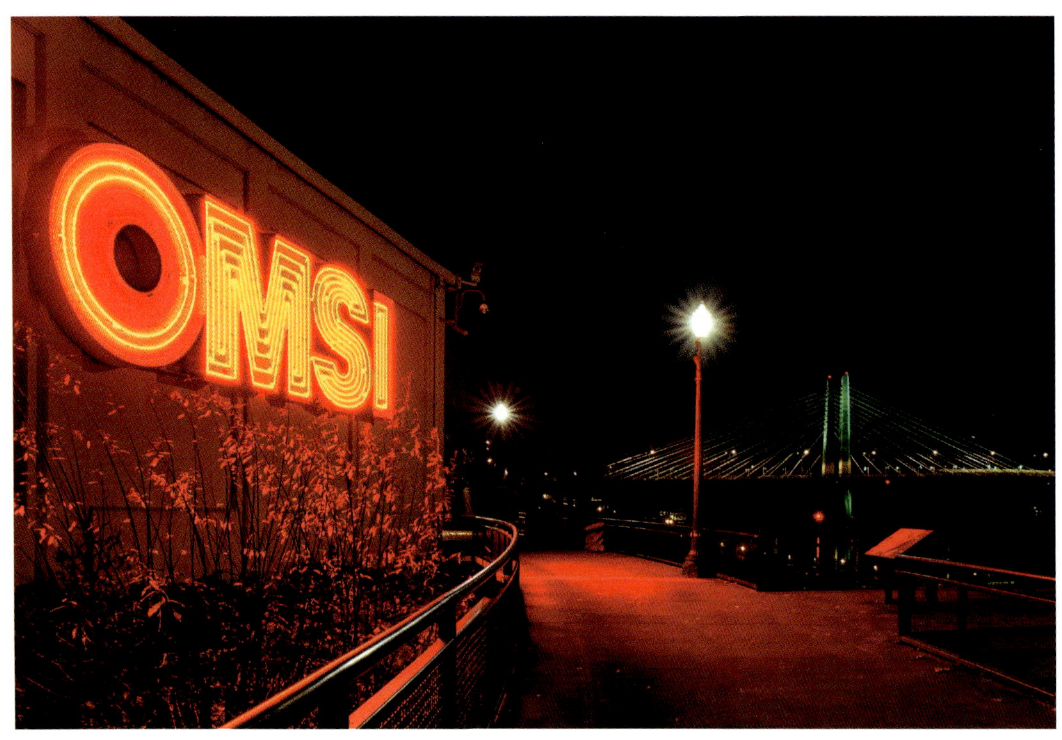


Oregon Museum of Science and Industry (OMSI) and Tilikum Crossing Bridge along Tom McCall Park on the Willamette River. *Photo by Barbara Tricarico*

Union Station, built in 1896. *Photo by Nomeca Hartwell*

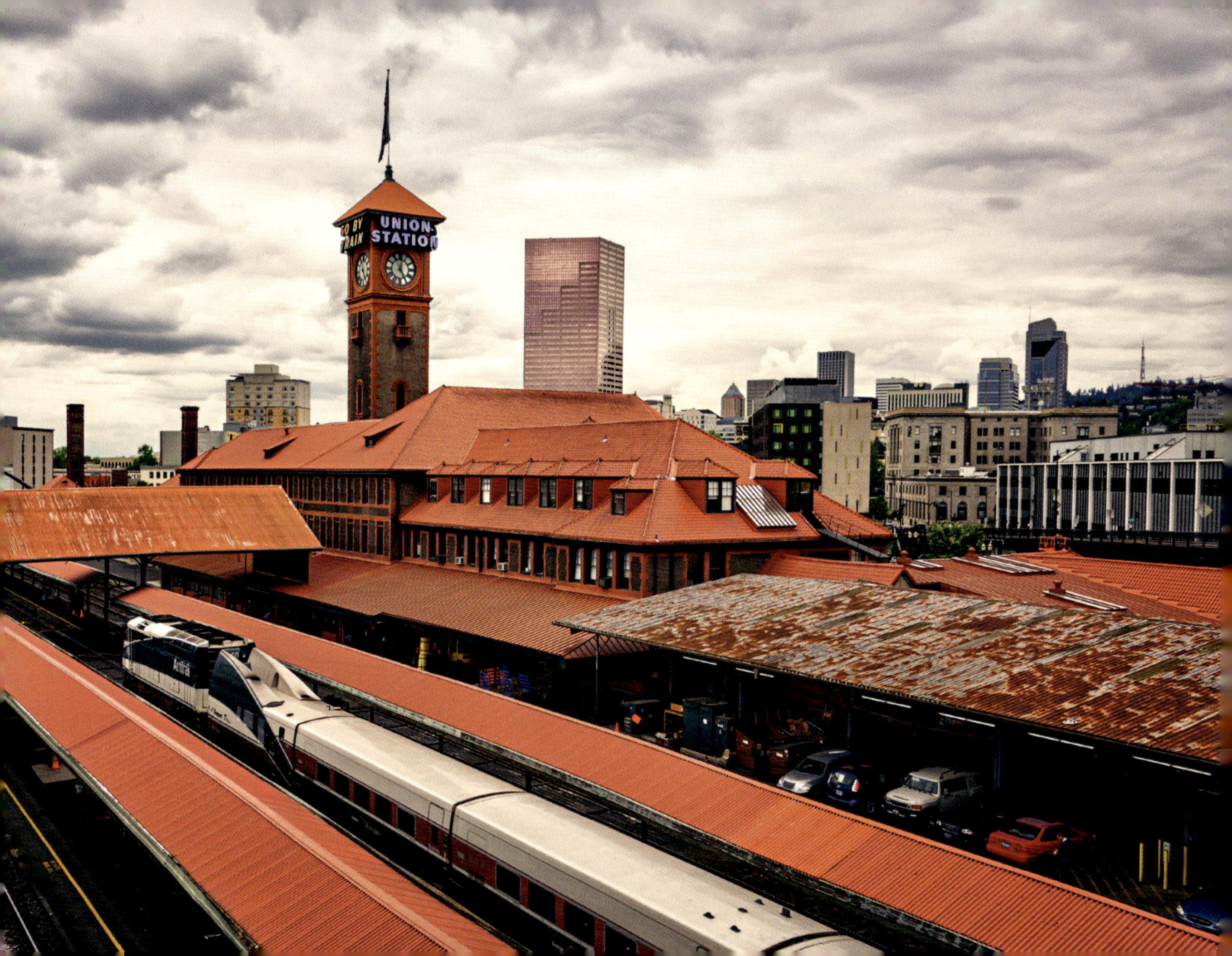
UNION
STATION

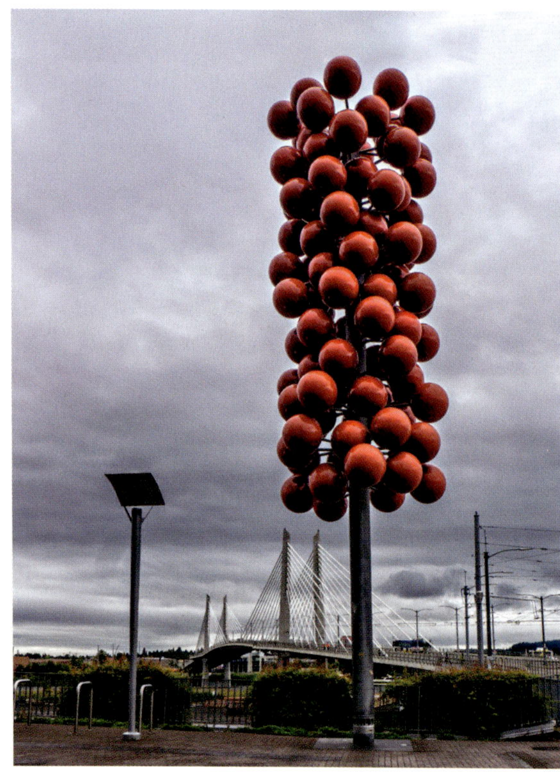

*Aril* sculpture by Christian Moeller at Collaborative Life Sciences Building (CLSB) at the South Waterfront, near the foot of the Tilikum Bridge. *Photo by Barbara Tricarico*

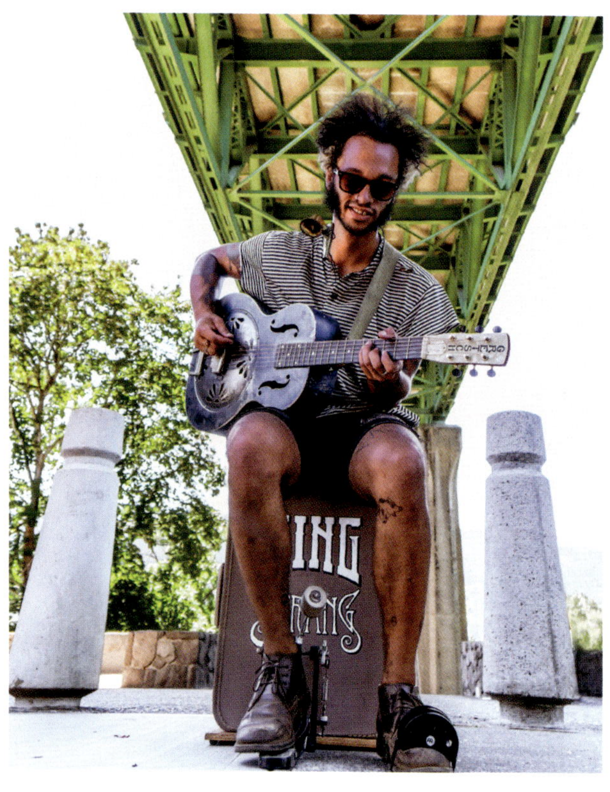

Musician Michael Flecha ("King Strang") entertains crowds under the St. John Bridge at the Cathedral Park Jazz Festival. *Photo by Cornelius Matteo*

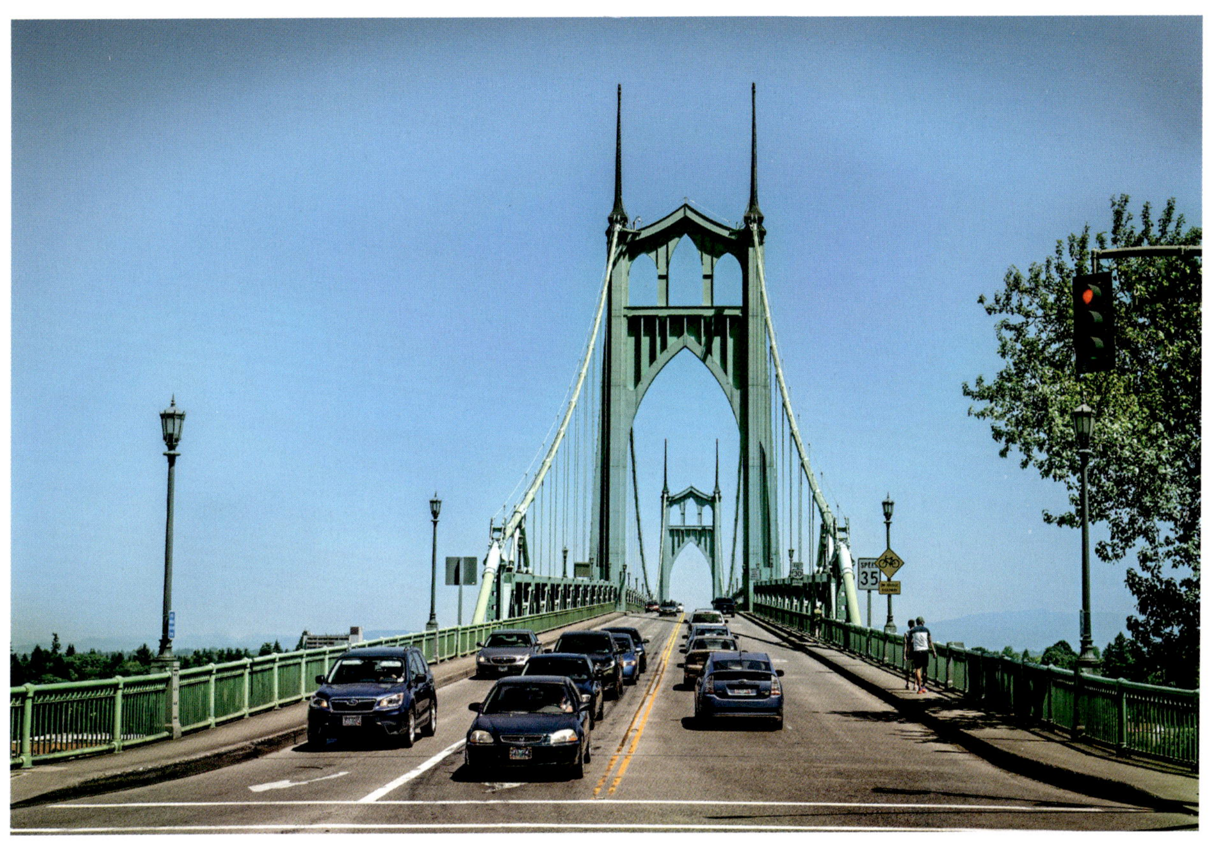


St. Johns Bridge, which opened in 1931, spans the Willamette River from Cathedral Park to Northwest Portland. *Photo by Barbara Tricarico*

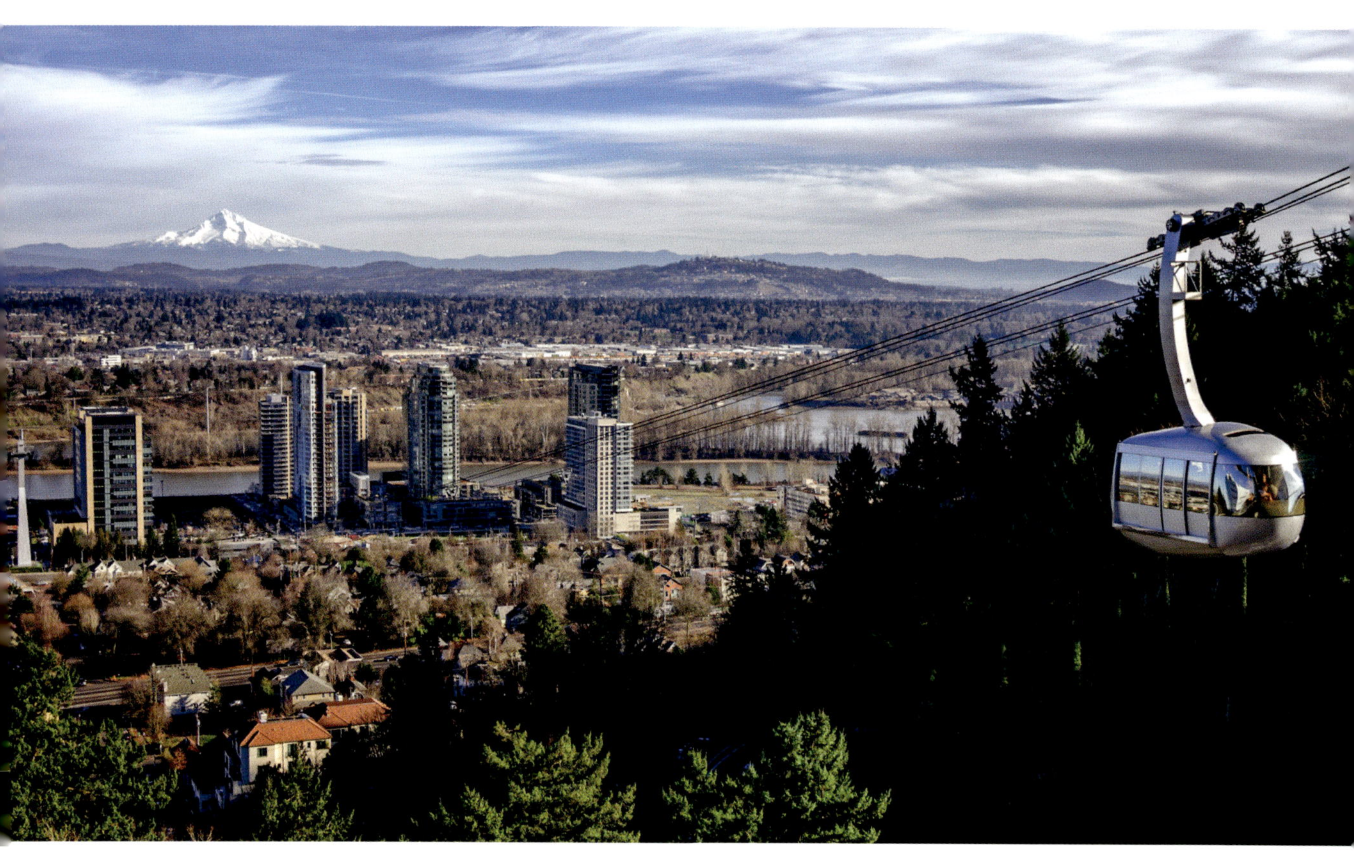

Portland Aerial Tram, with Mount Hood in background.
*Photo by Barbara Tricarico*

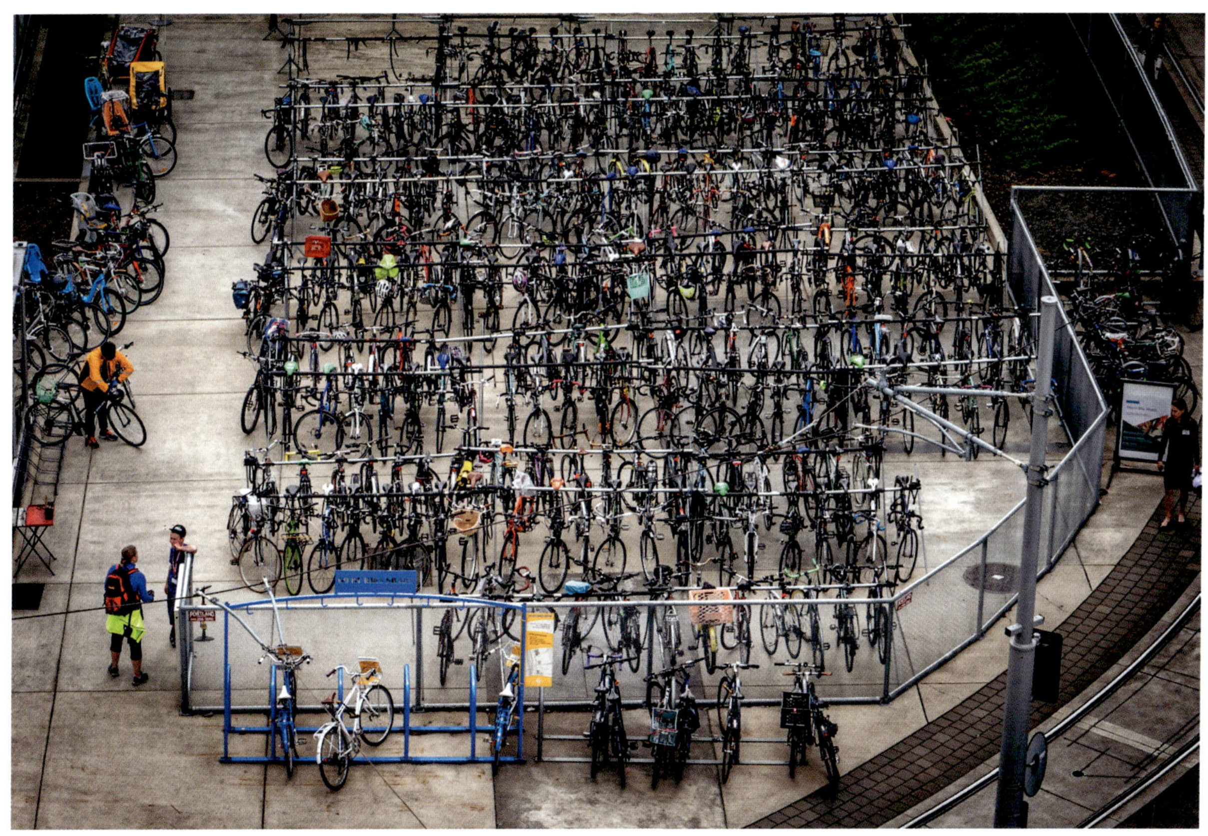

Go By Bike lot under the Portland Aerial Tram. It is the largest bike valet in North America. *Photo by Barbara Tricarico*

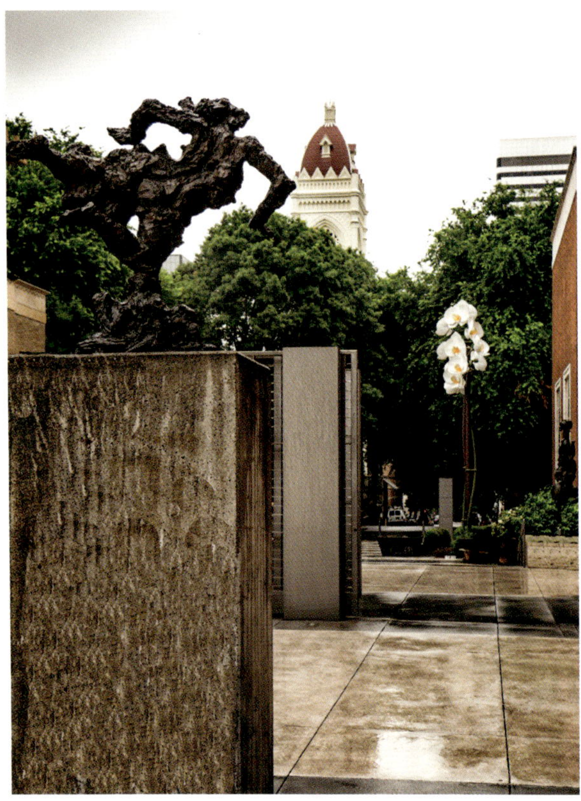

Courtyard, Portland Art Museum, the oldest art museum in the Pacific Northwest, founded in 1892. First Congregational Church in background, founded in 1851. *Photo by Barbara Tricarico*

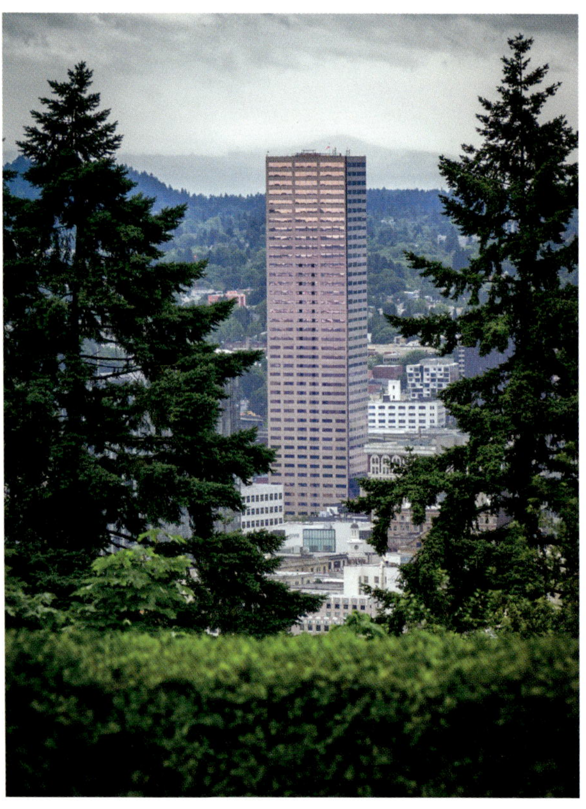

"Big Pink" (US Bancorp Tower) from the Portland Japanese Garden. *Photo by Barbara Tricarico*

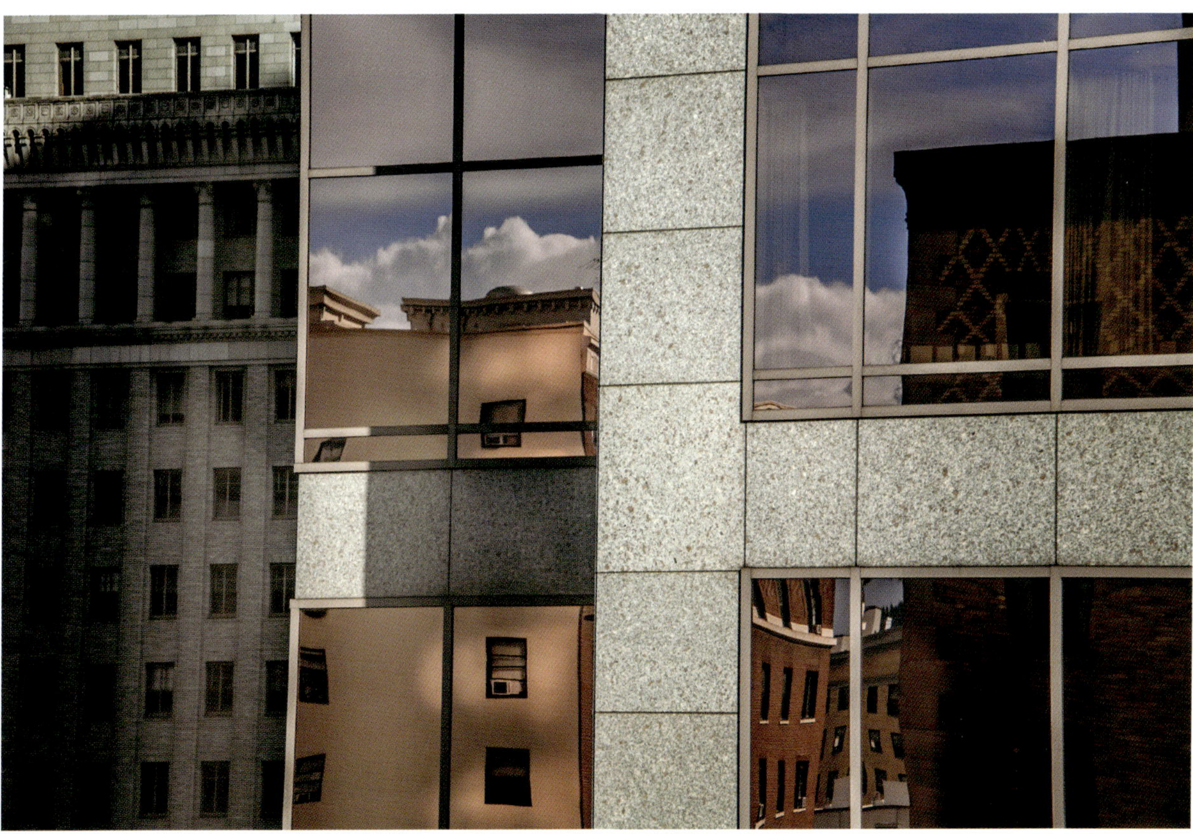

Portland architecture. *Photo by Diana Standing*

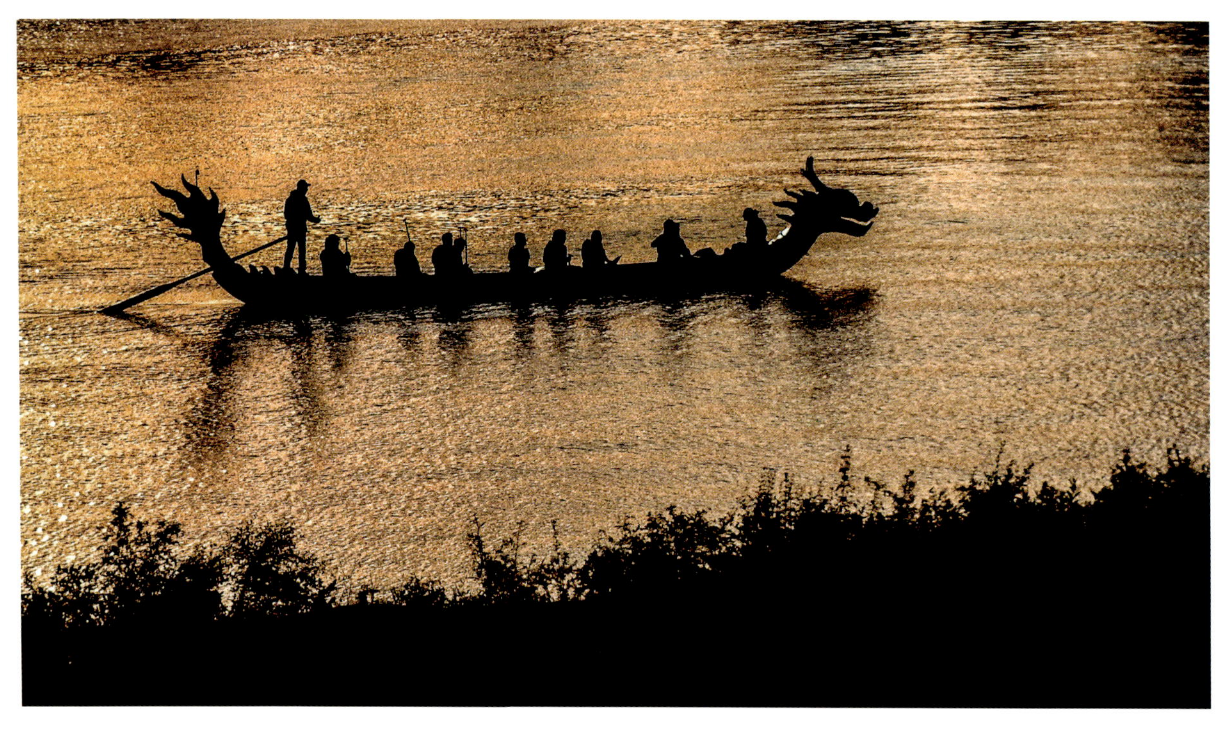

Dragon boat on the Willamette River. *Photo by Charles Hillestad*

Ross Island Bridge. *Photo by Charles Hillestad*

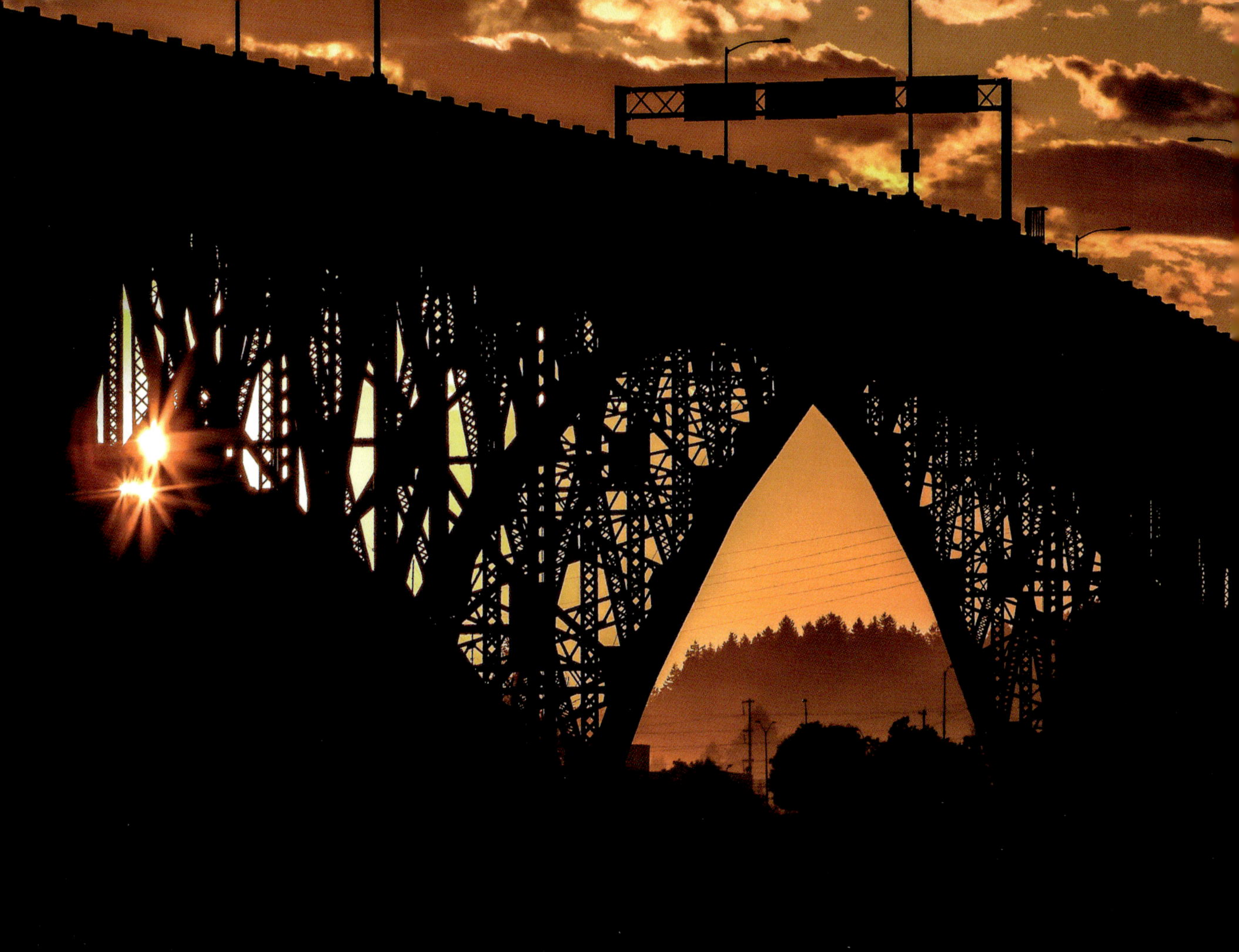

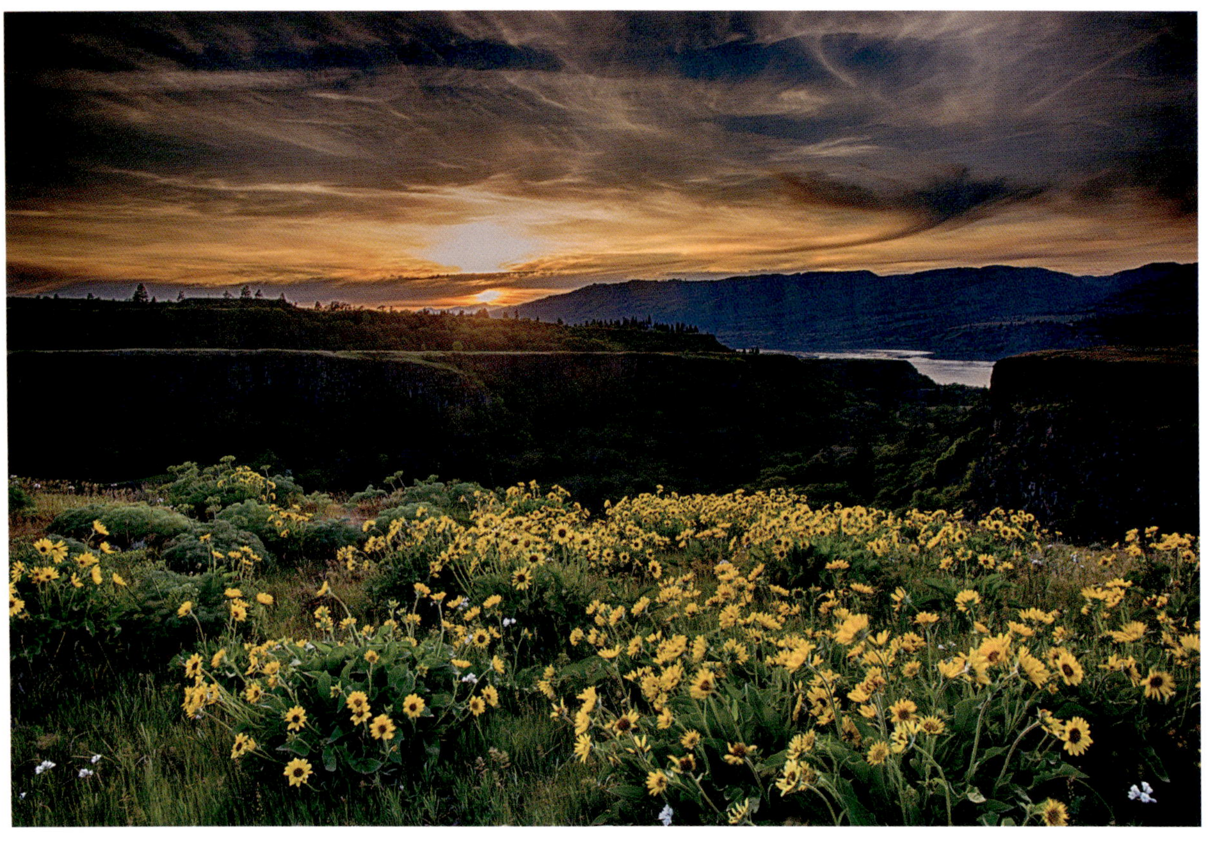

Wildflowers at Rowena Crest, Columbia River Gorge.
*Photo by Terry Tuttle*

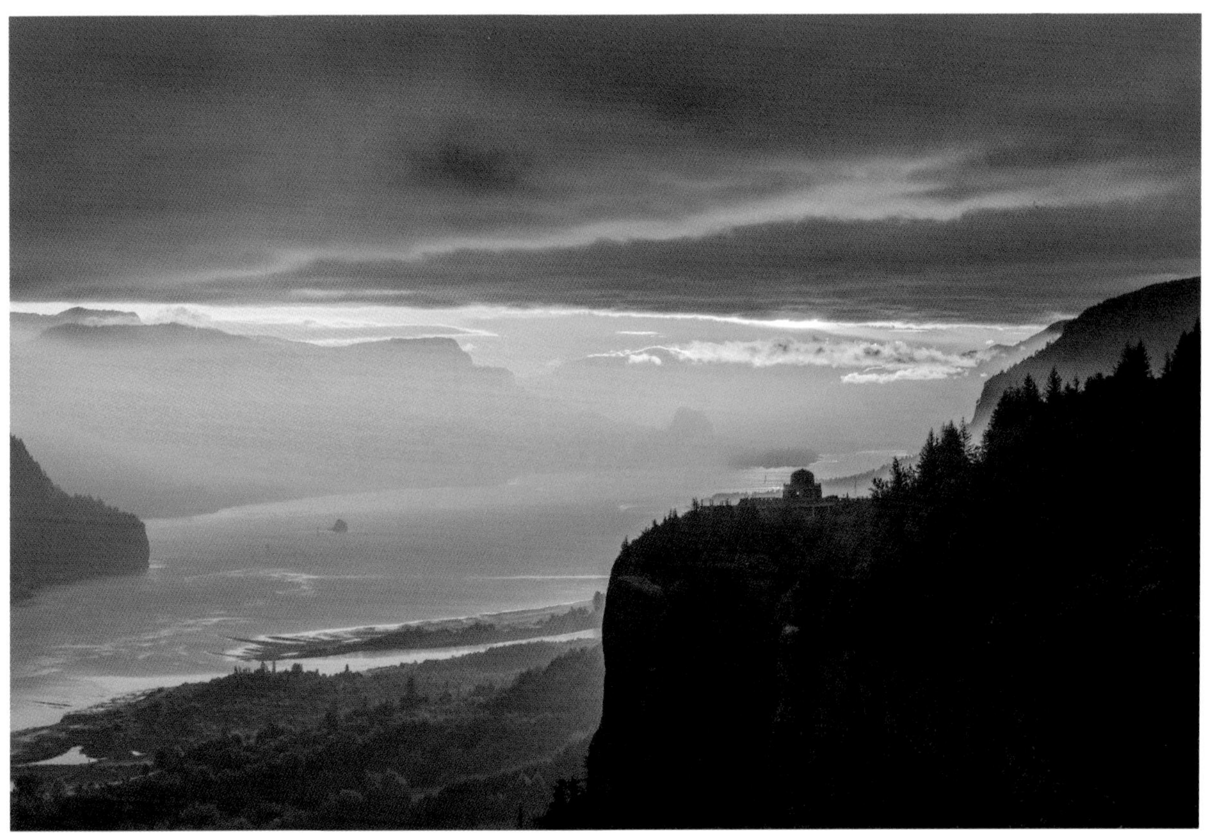



Columbia River Gorge sunrise. Vista House in foreground.
*Photo by Vldn Taylor*

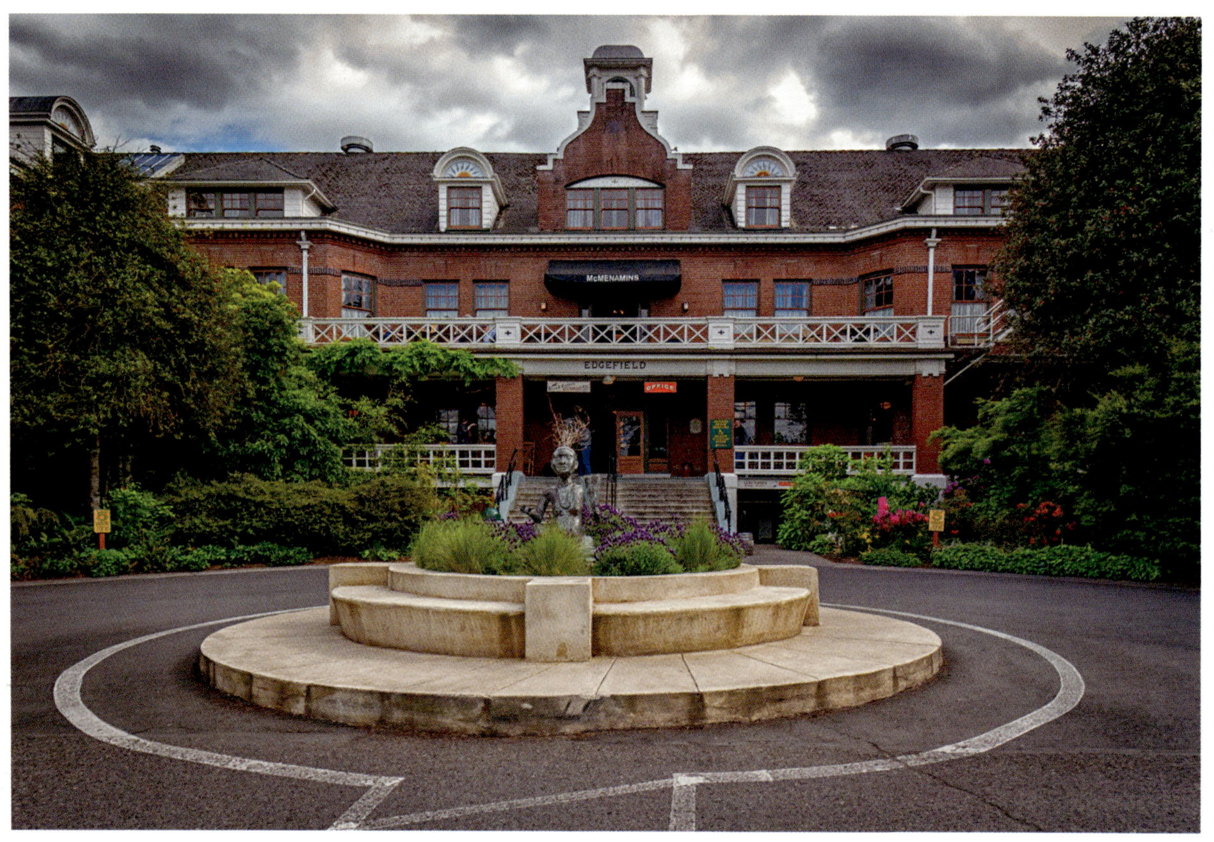


McMenamins Edgefield Hotel, Troutdale. It was built in 1911 as the Multnomah County Poor Farm. *Photo by Barbara Tricarico*

Columbia River Gorge. *Photo by Vivian McAleavey*

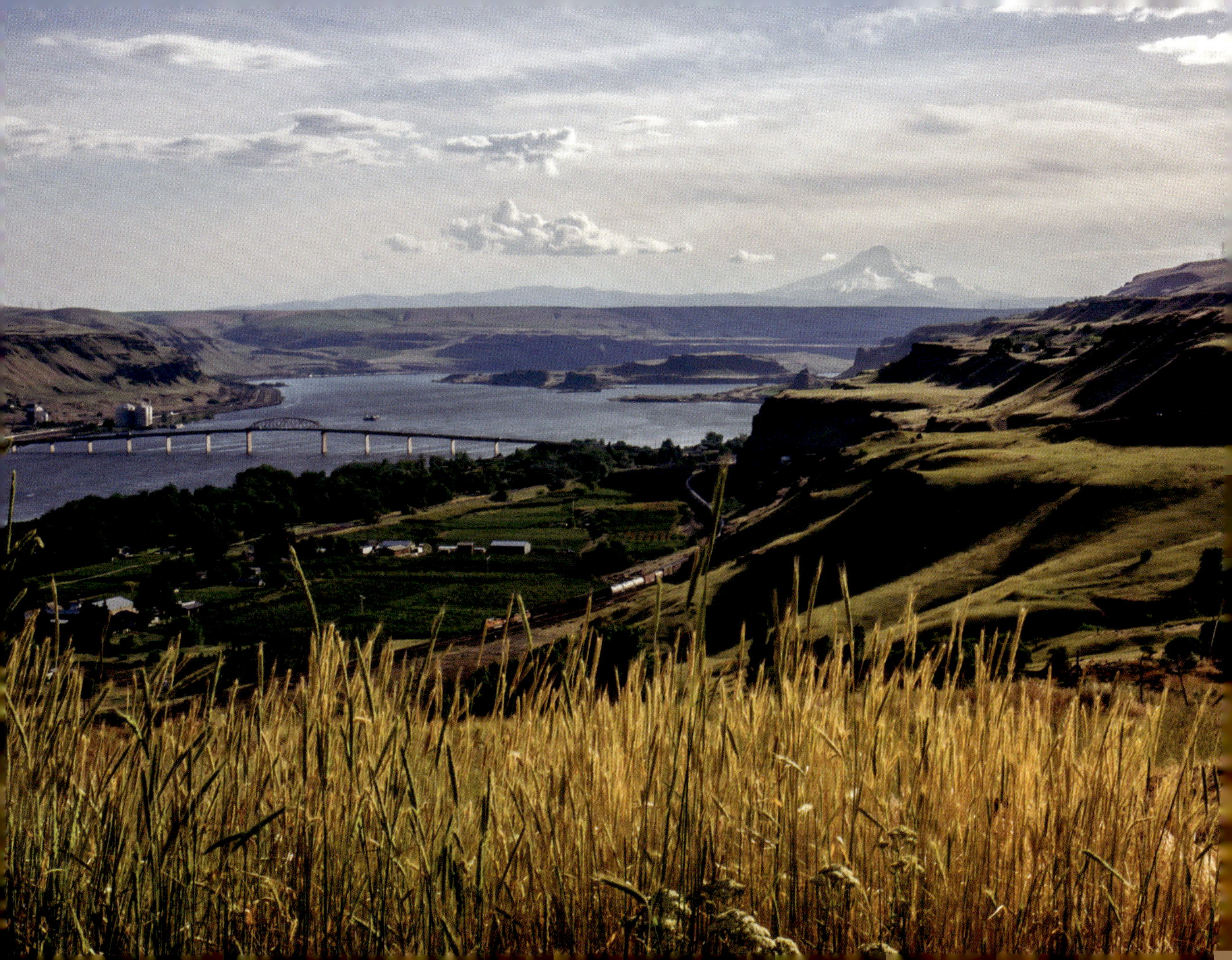

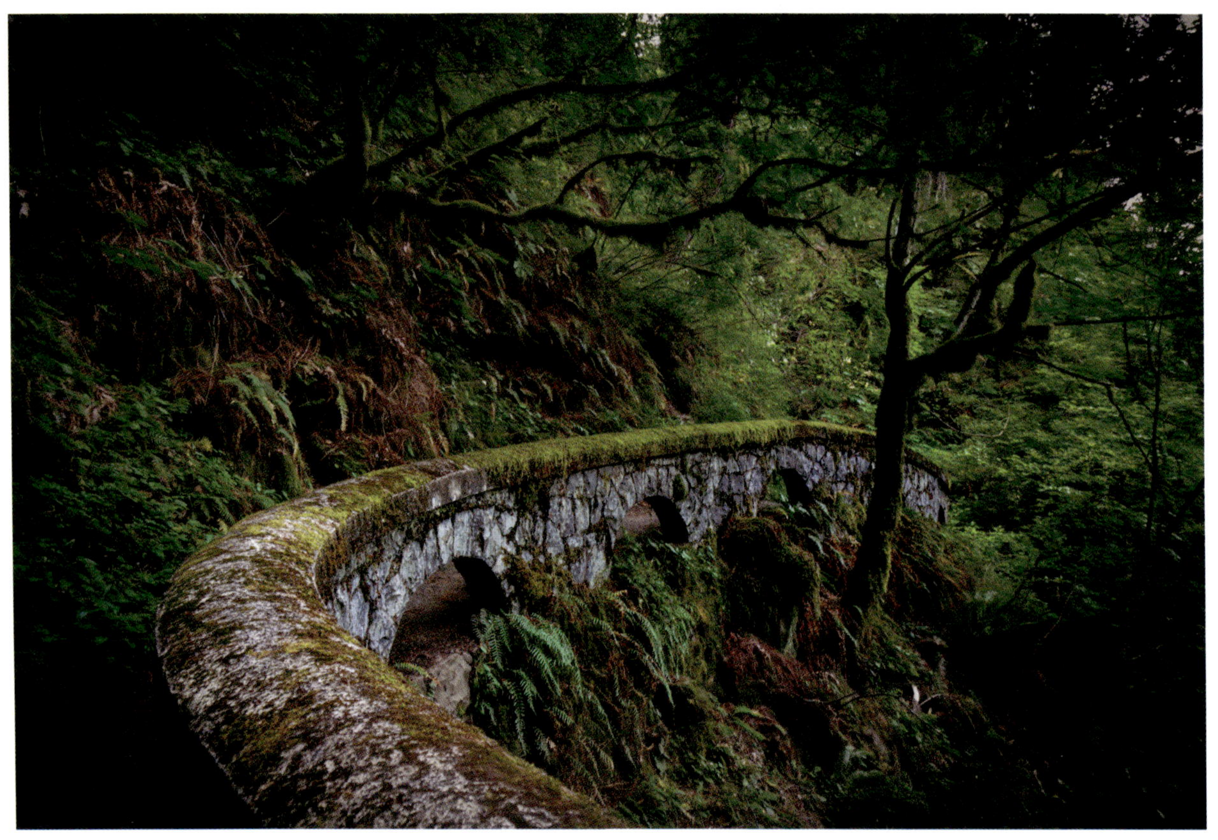

Trail to Shepperd's Dell Falls, Columbia River Gorge. *Photo by Alana Lynn Starkweather*

Multnomah Falls roadway. *Photo by Bob Palermini*

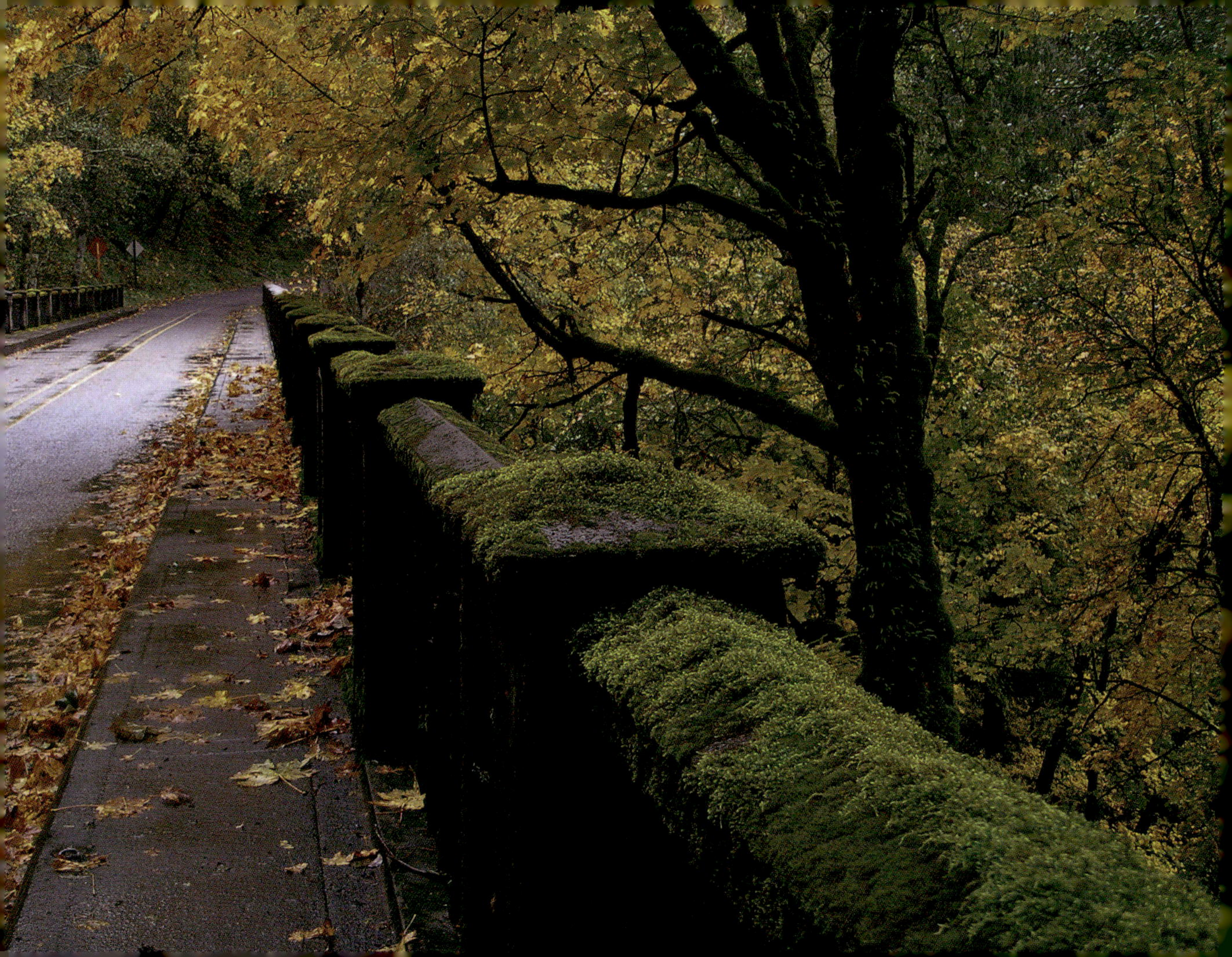

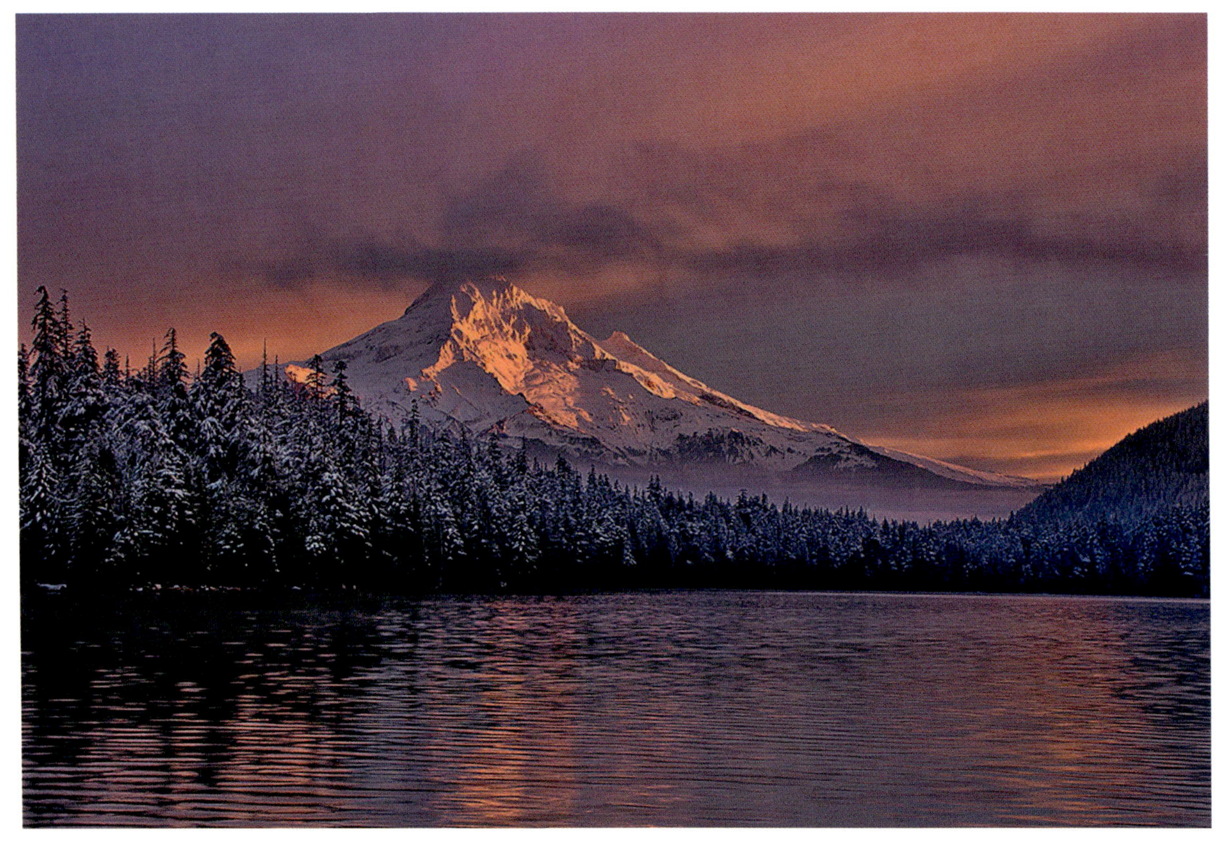

Mount Hood. *Photo by Clem Paslack*

Milky Way over Mount Hood and Lost Lake. *Photo by Clem Paslack*

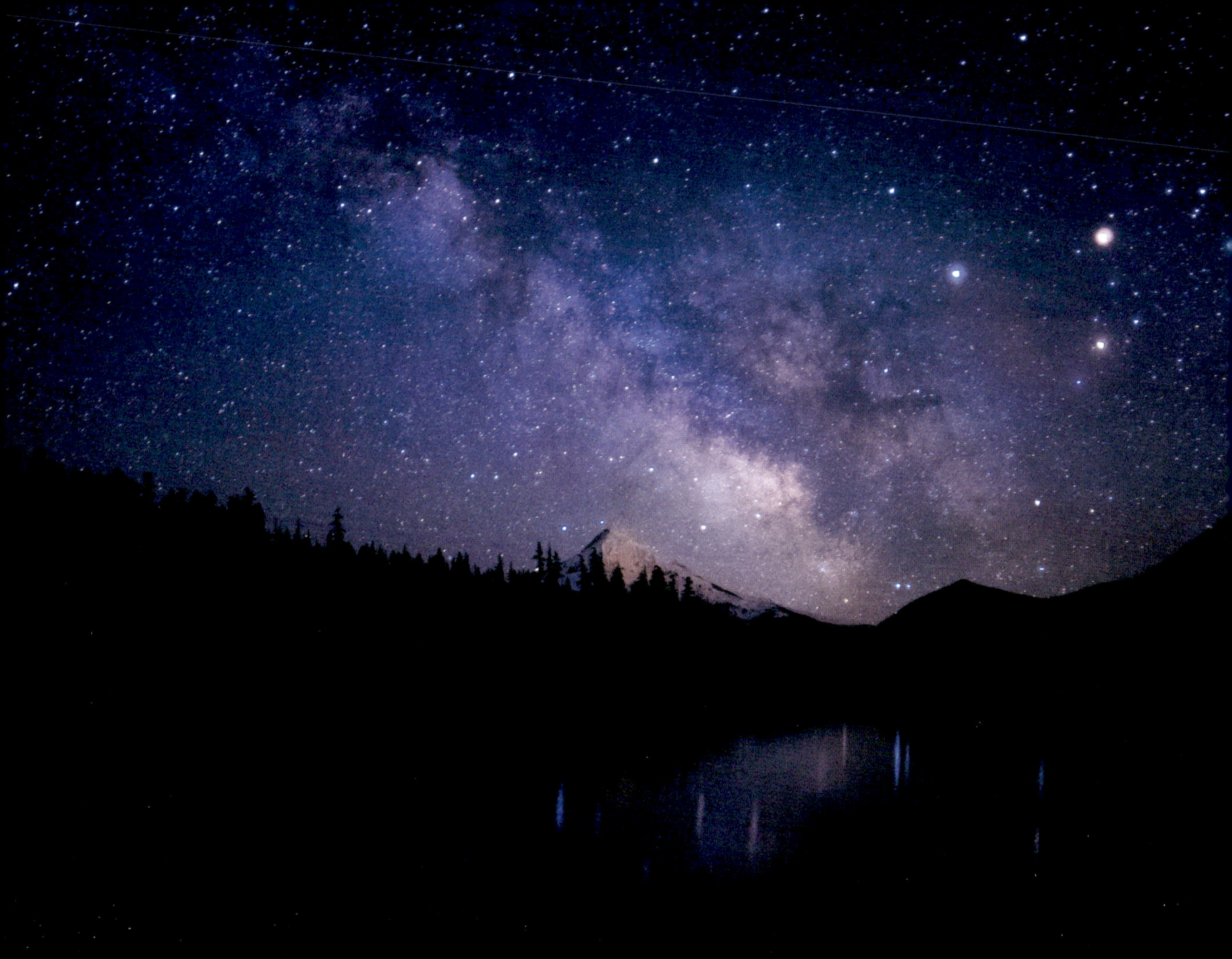

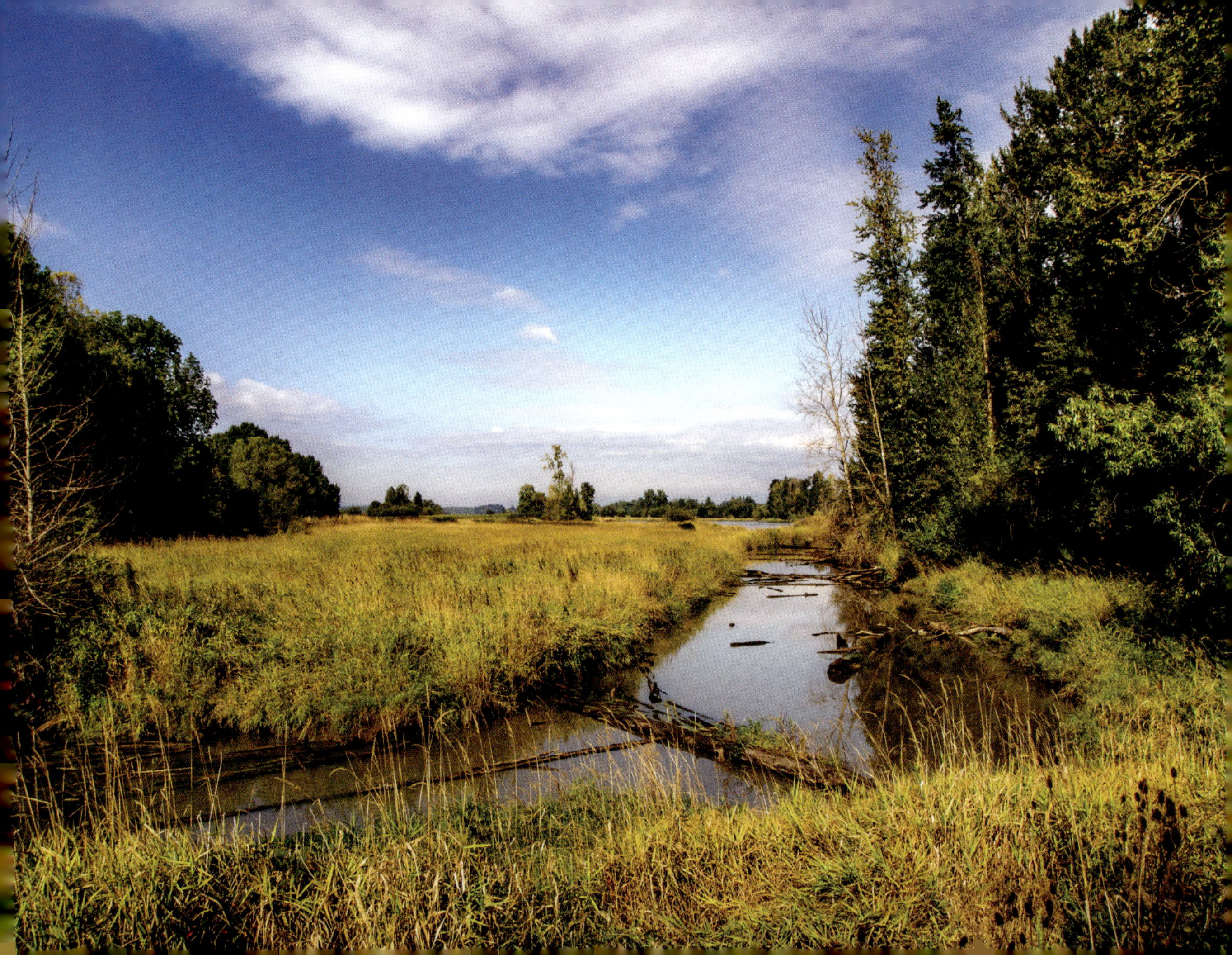

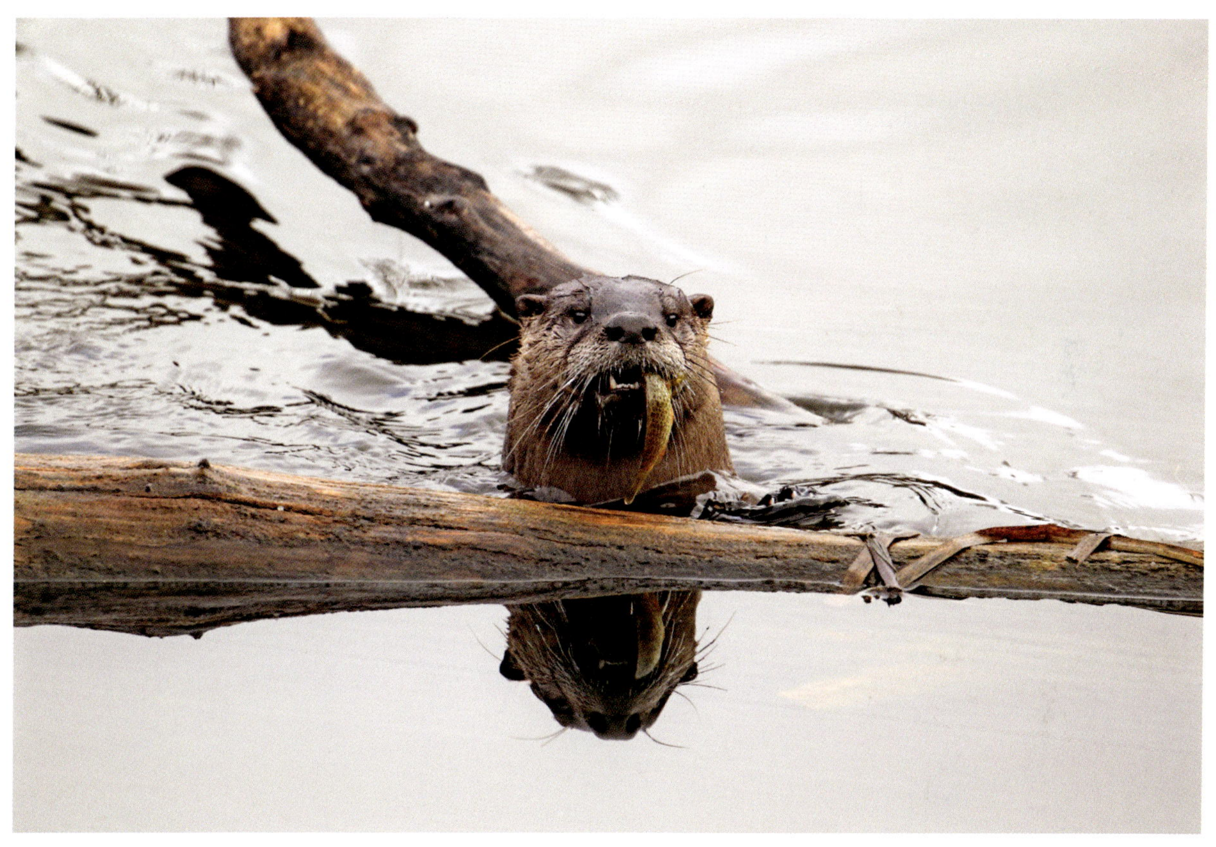



Sauvie Island, a wildlife refuge surrounded by abundant farmland, is just outside Portland. It is the largest island along the Columbia River. *Photo by Nick Viani*

River otter. *Photo by Dan Elster*

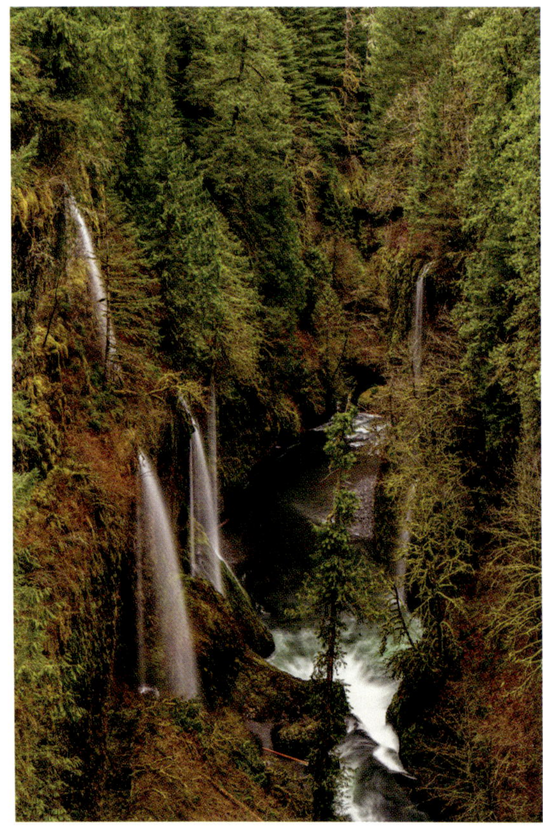

Weeping Walls, Eagle Creek Trail, Columbia River Gorge.
*Photo by Vldn Taylor*

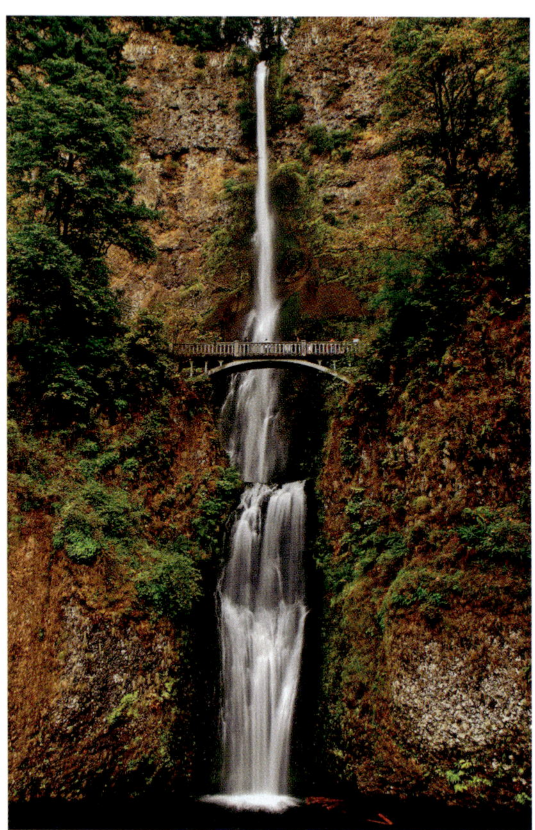

Multnomah Falls is the tallest waterfall in Oregon at 620 feet, and the most visited recreation site in the Northwest.
*Photo by Jay Newman*

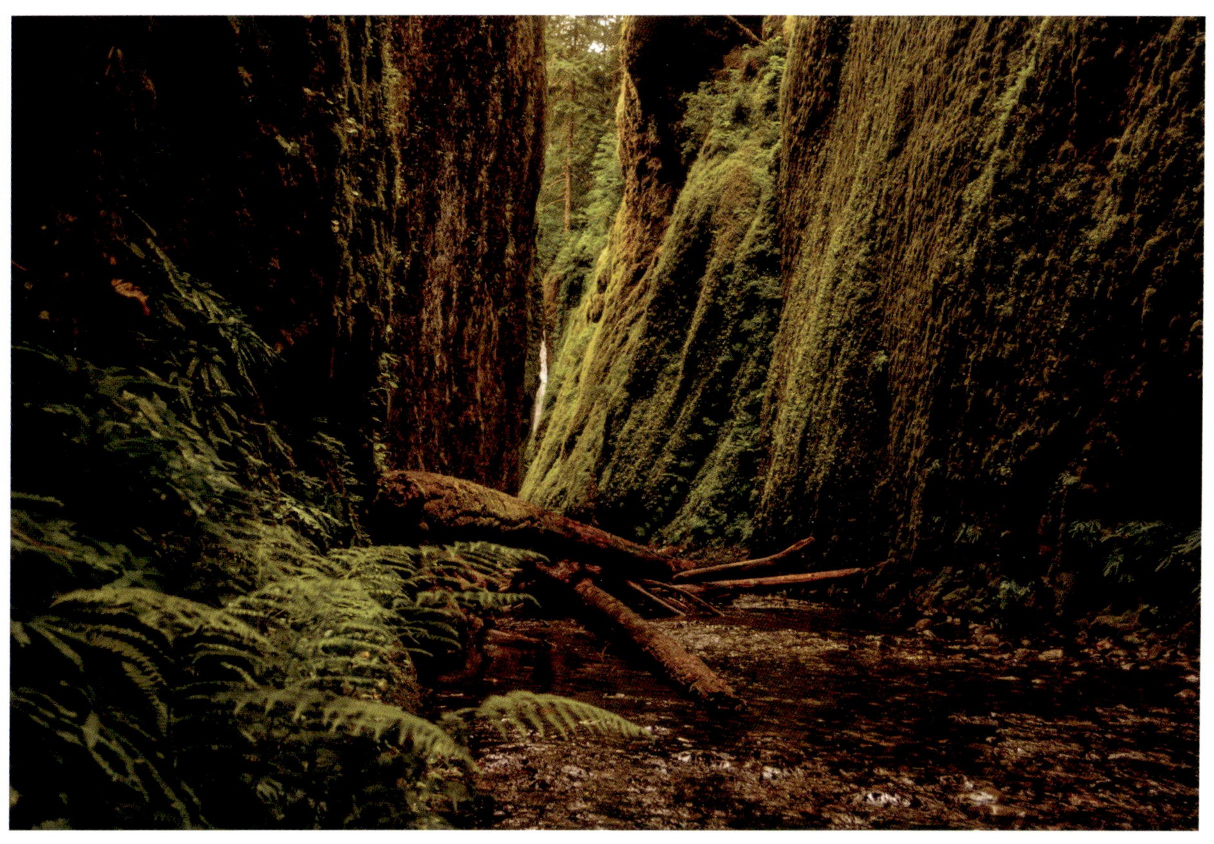

Oneonta Gorge. *Photo by Hans Stroo*

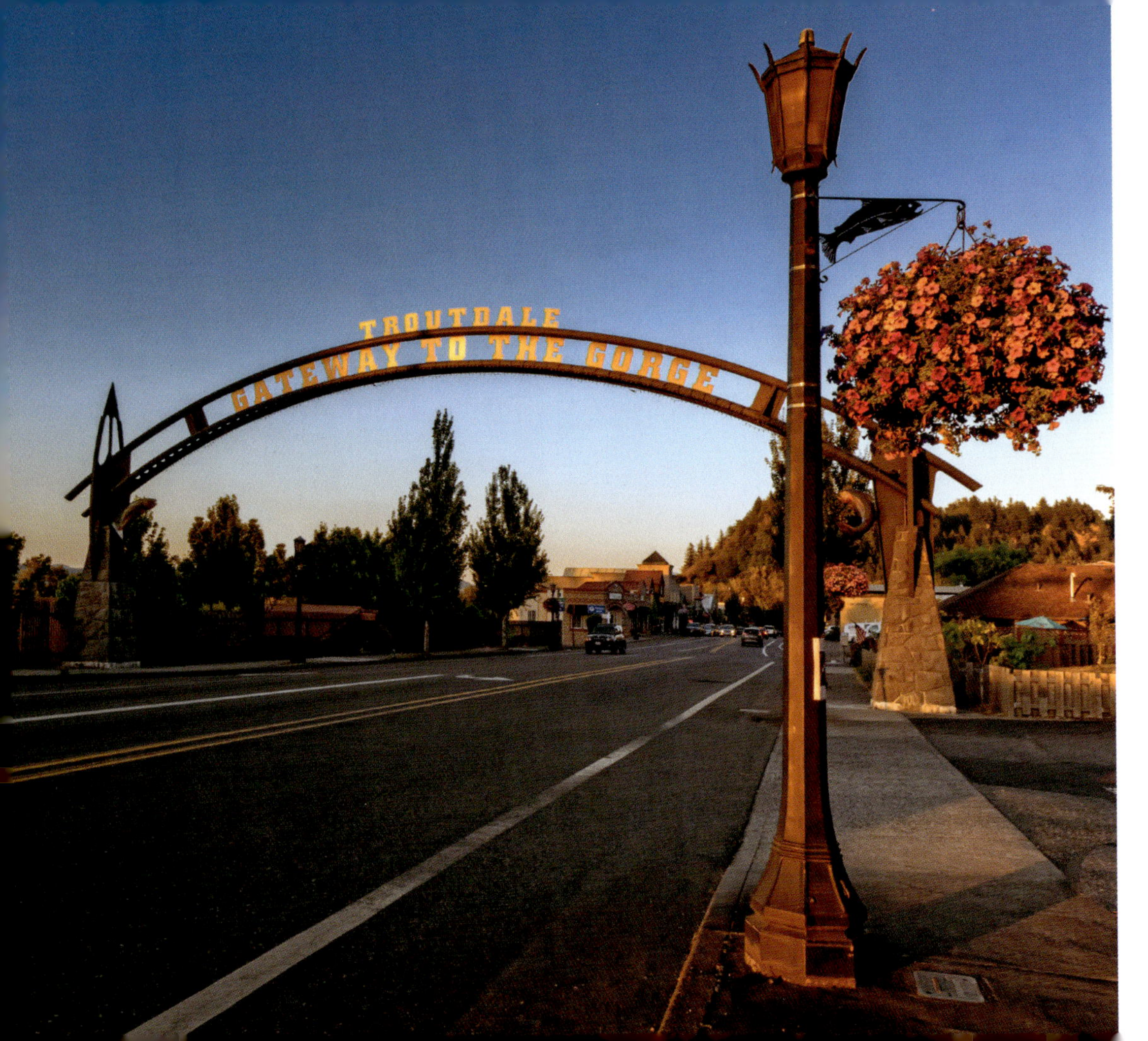
TROUTDALE
GATEWAY TO THE GORGE

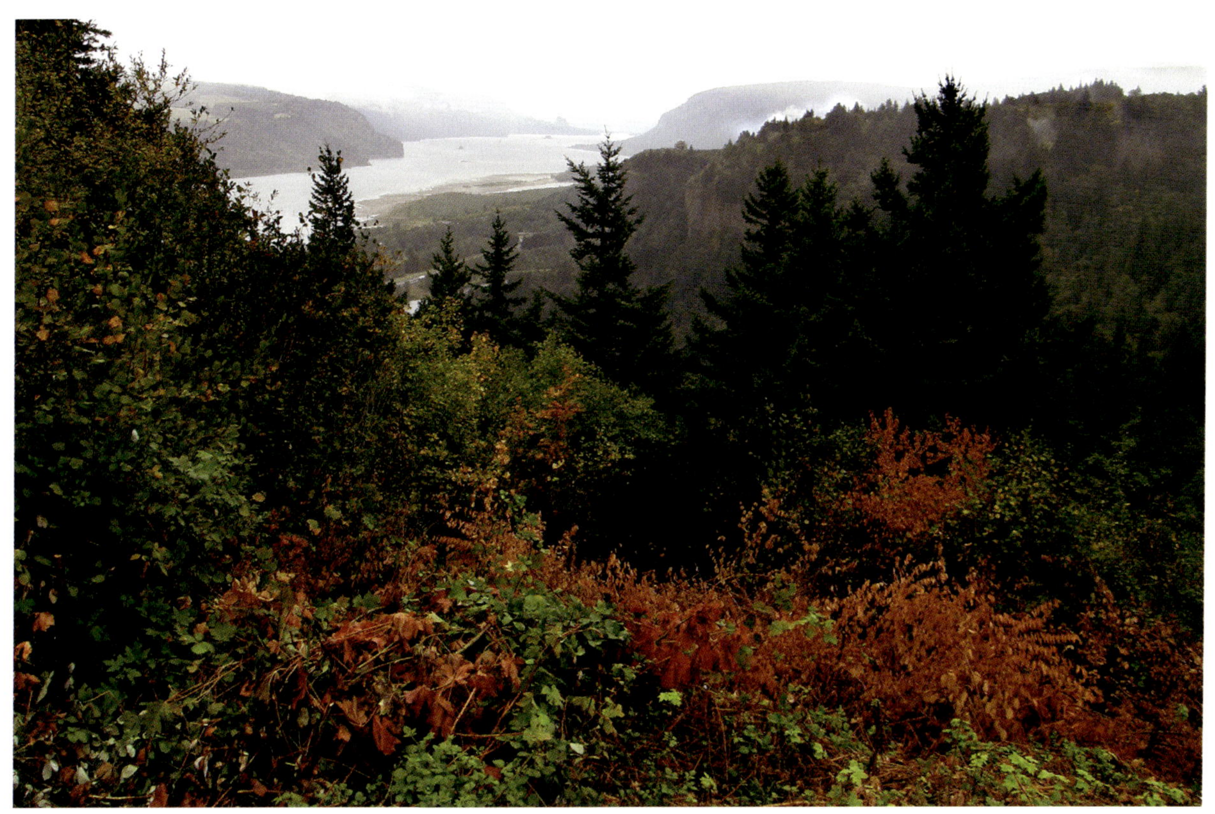



Troutdale, Gateway to the Gorge. The sculpture by Rip Caswell was installed in 2010 to commemorate the 100th birthday of Troutdale. *Photo by Barbara Tricarico*

Columbia River Gorge overview. *Photo by Charles Hillestad*

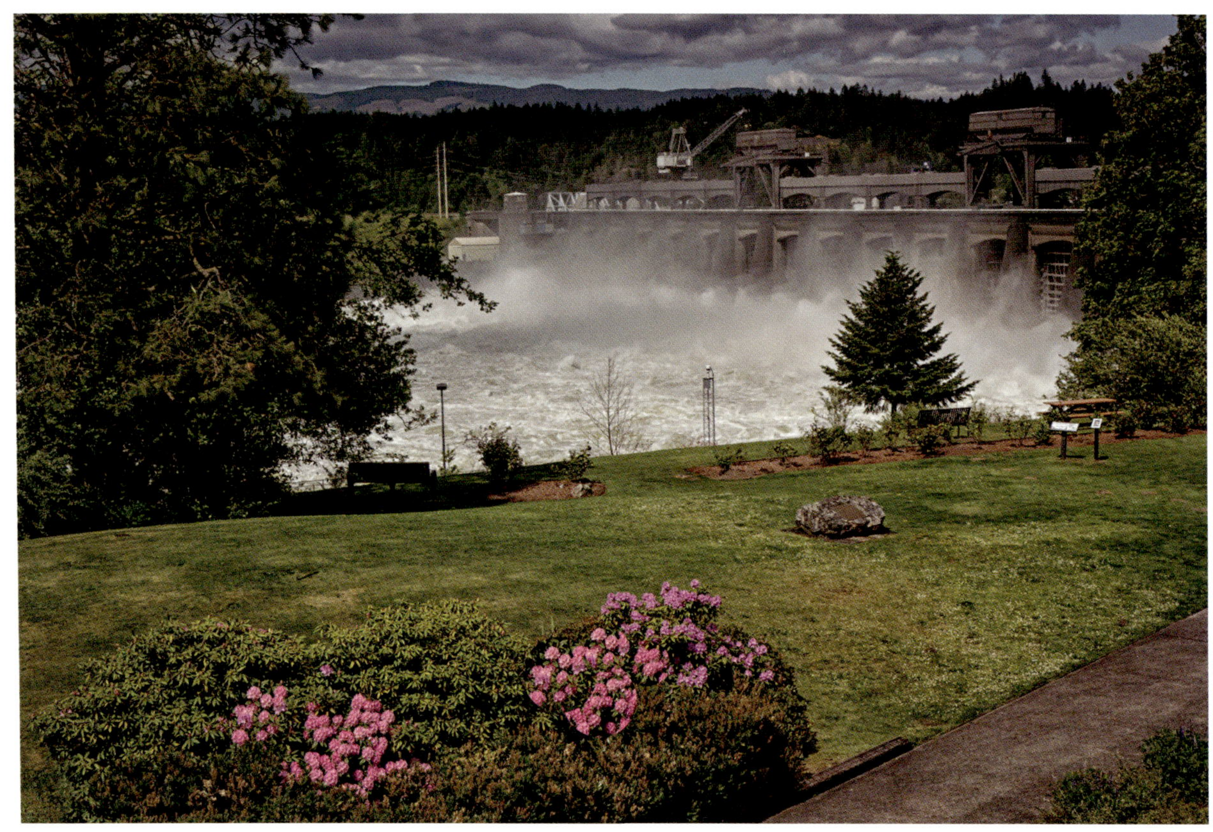

Bonneville Dam. *Photo by Barbara Tricarico*

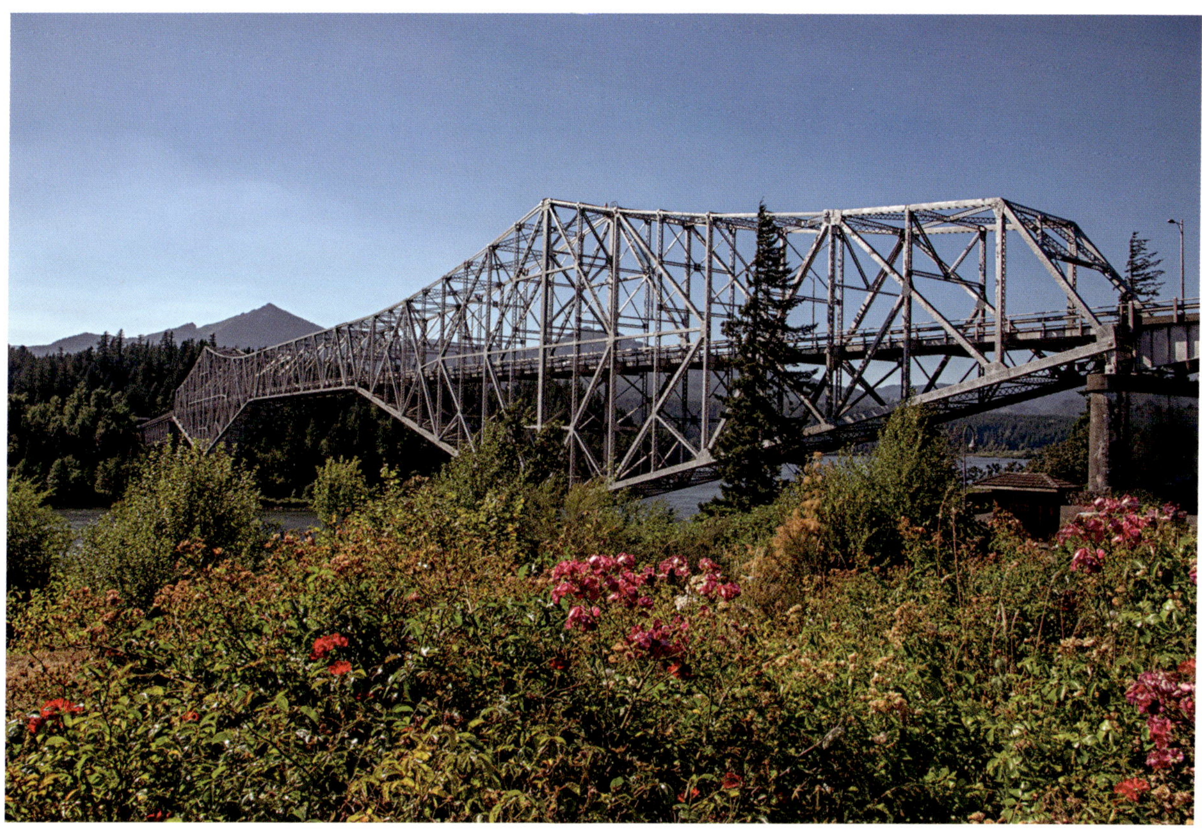



Bridge of the Gods. Originally named by Native Americans for a natural dam, this steel toll bridge over the Columbia River was built in 1926. *Photo by Barbara Tricarico*

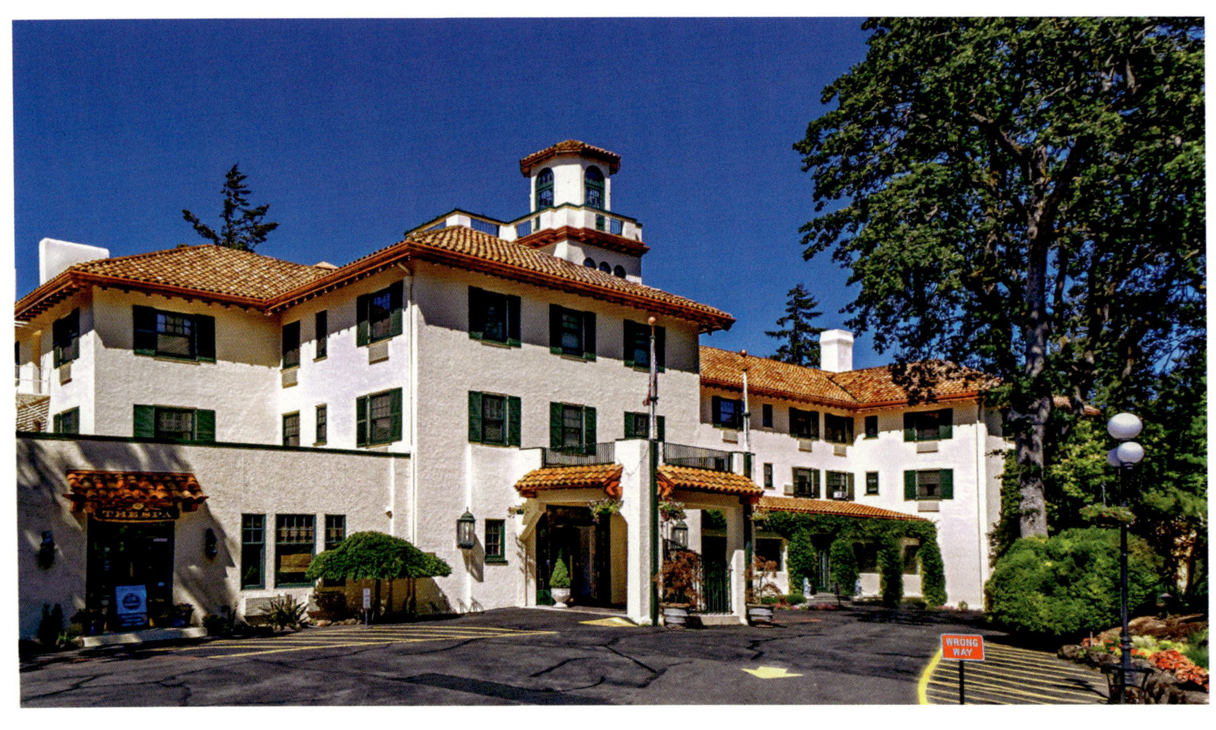


The Columbia Gorge Hotel in Hood River opened in 1921. *Photo by Cornelius Matteo*

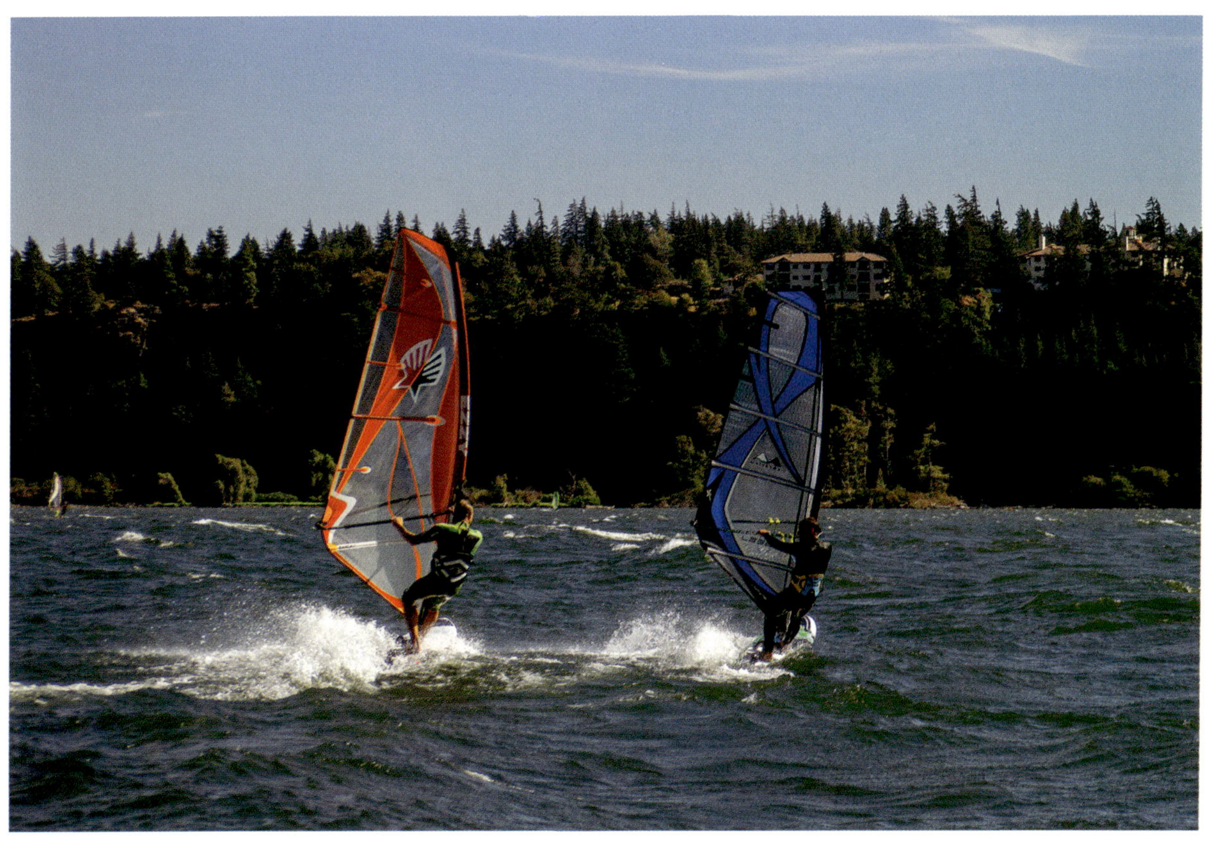

Windsurfing on the Columbia River Gorge. *Photo by Vldn Taylor*

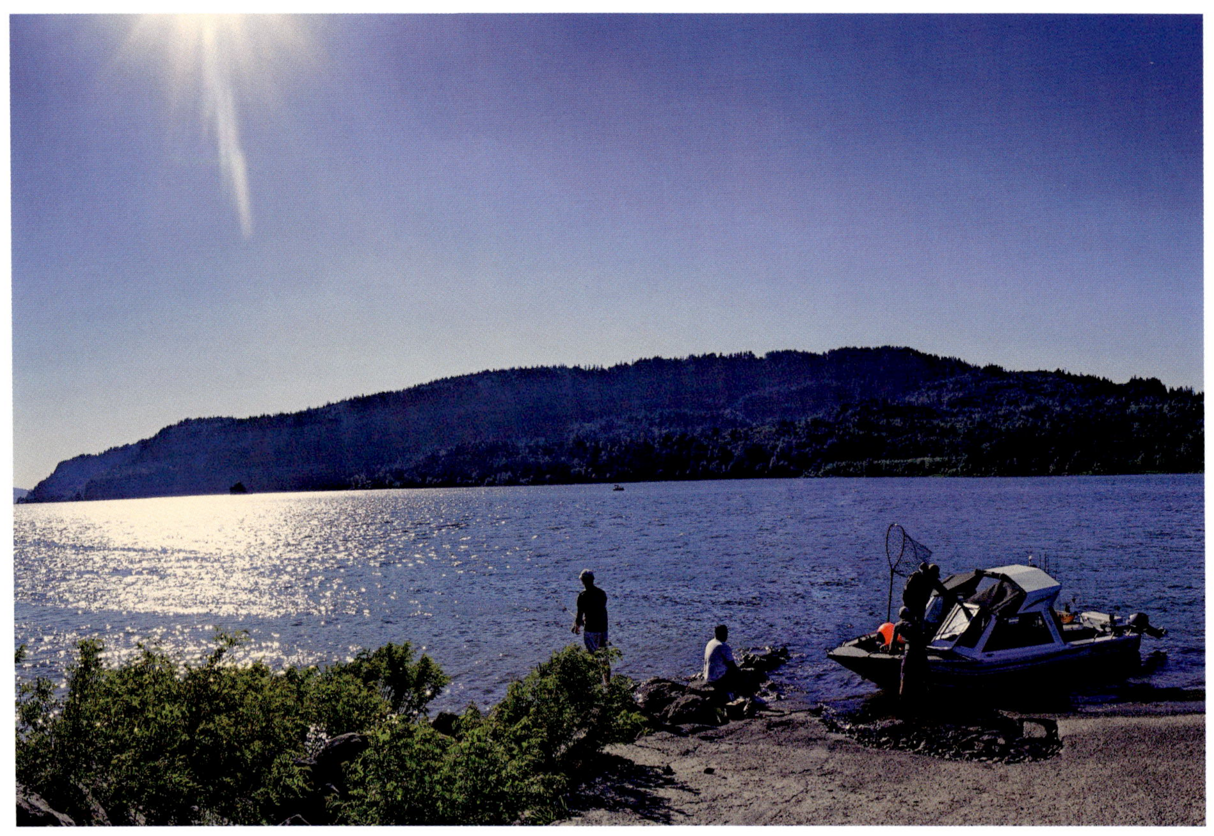

Fishing on the Columbia River. *Photo by Cornelius Matteo*

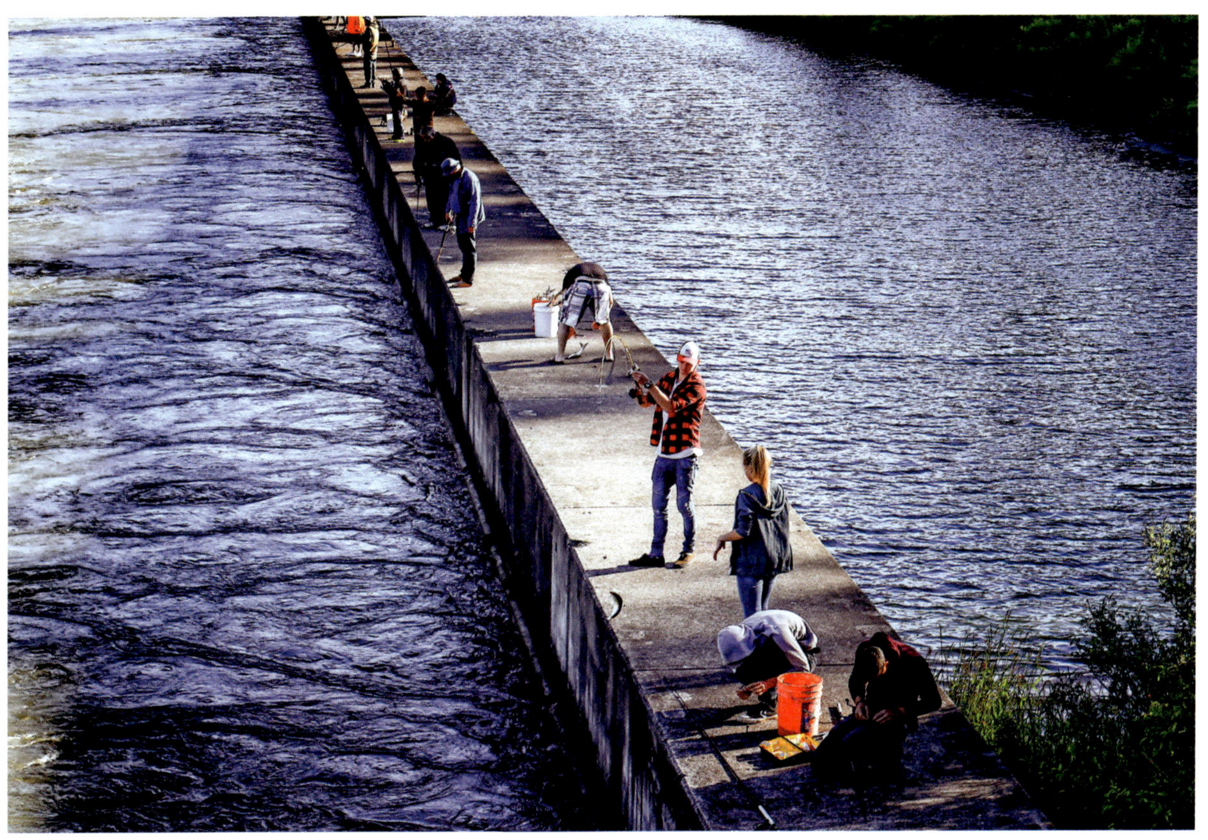

Shad fishing at Cascade Locks. *Photo by Terry Fisher*

74

Columbia River Gorge windsurfers. *Photo by Vldn Taylor*

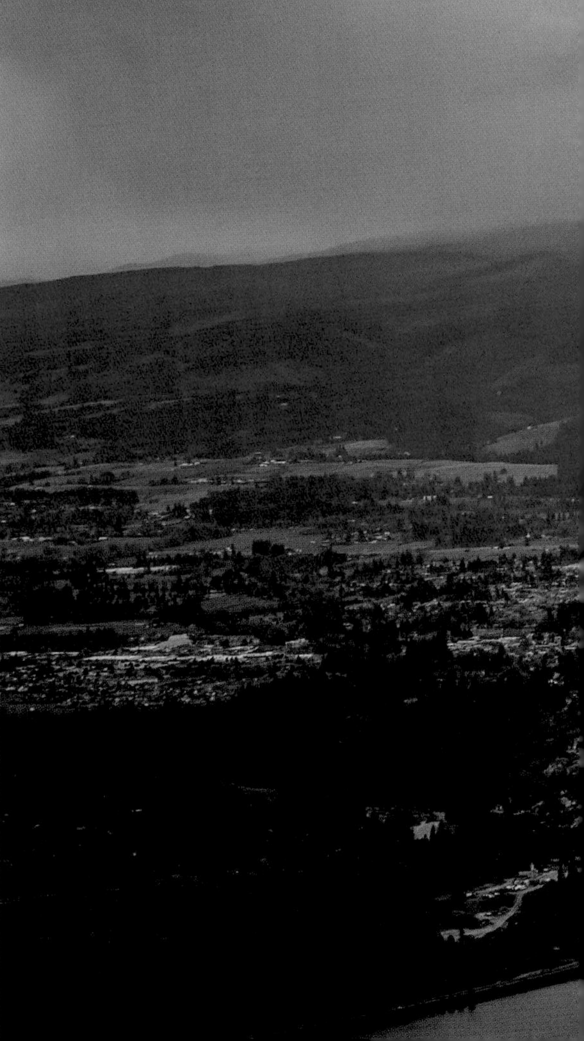

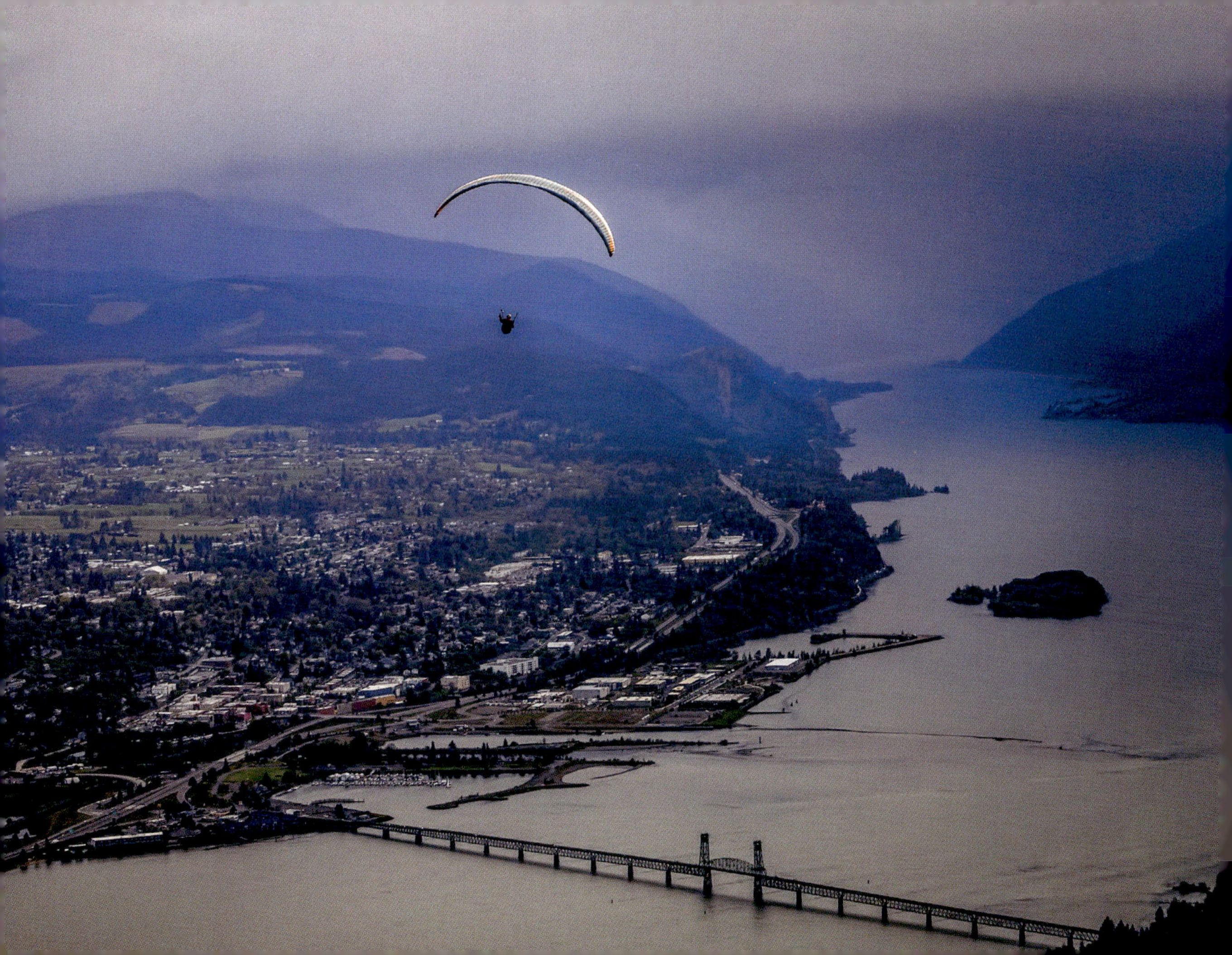

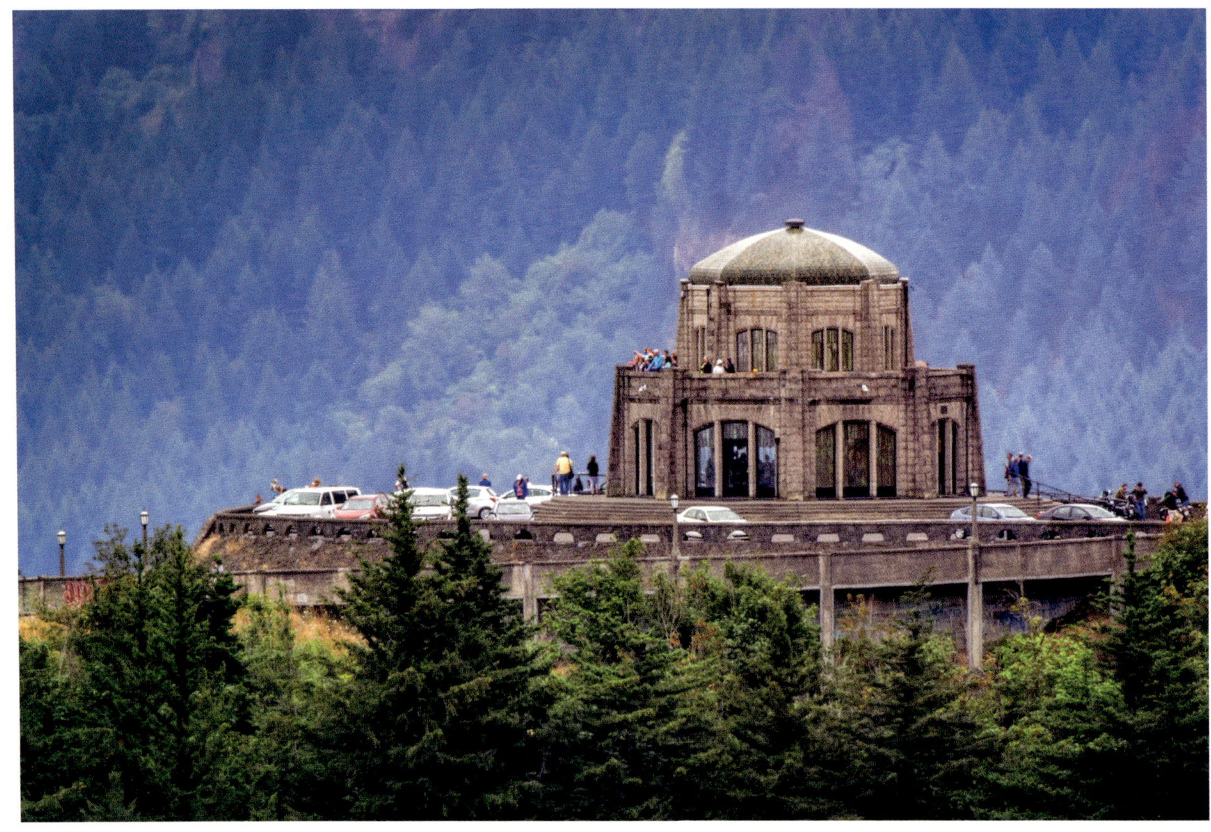

Vista House juts out prominently along the Historic Columbia River Highway about 733 feet above the Columbia River. It was completed in 1918. *Photo by Barbara Tricarico*

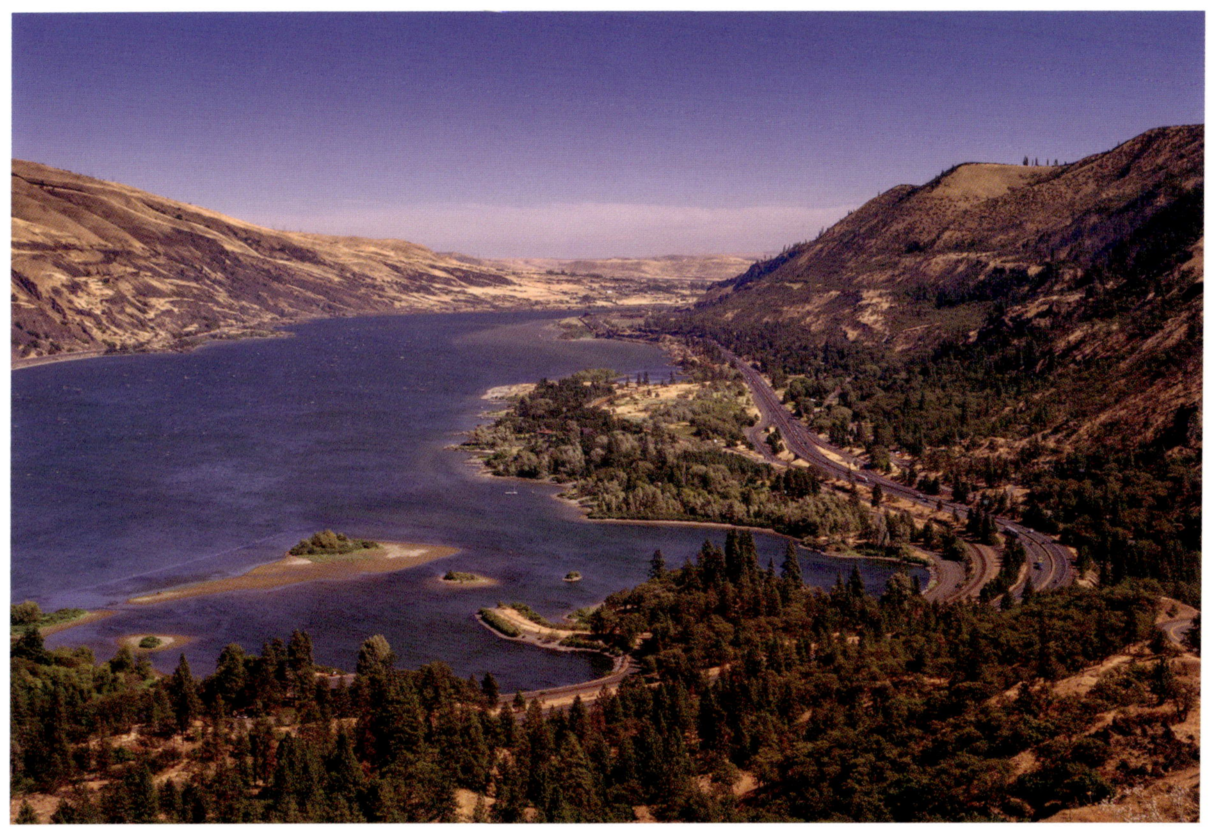

Historic Columbia River Highway. The first planned scenic highway in the United States was begun in 1913 and stretches 75 miles from Troutdale to the Dalles. *Photo by Ken Deveney*

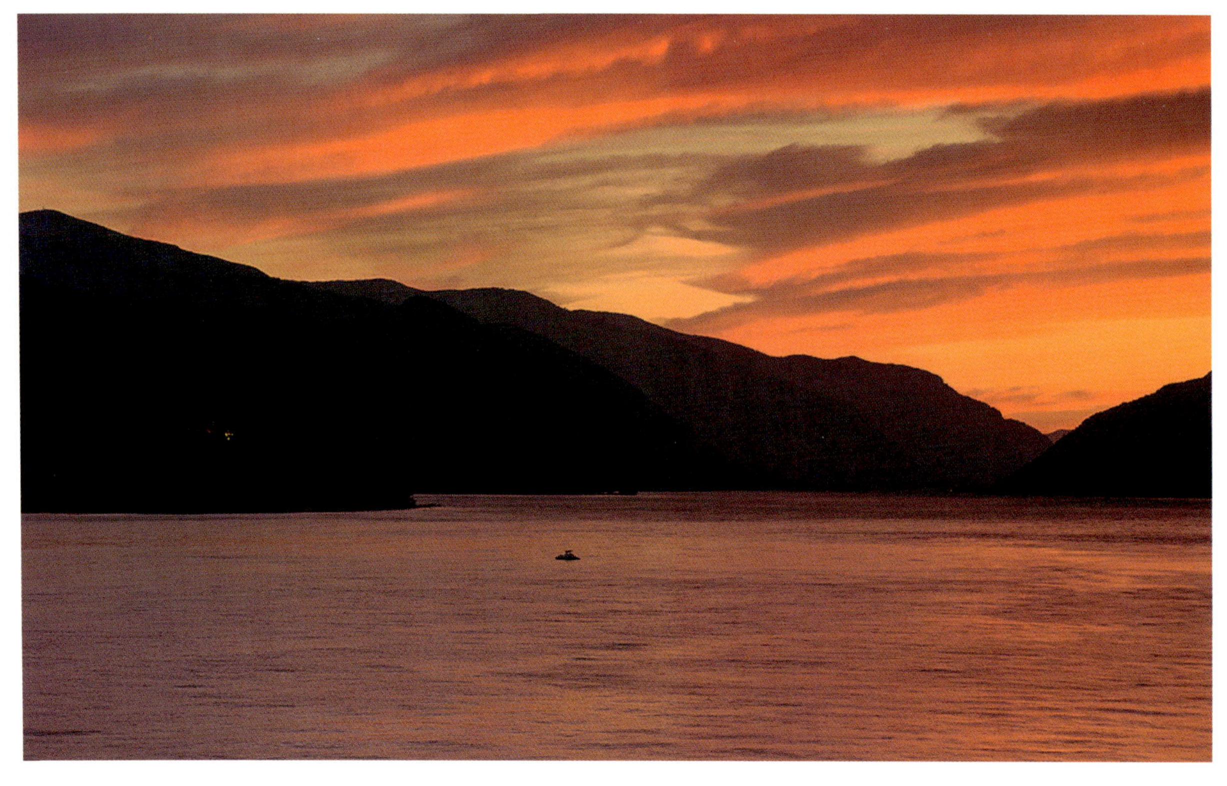

Columbia River Gorge. *Photo by Clem Paslack*

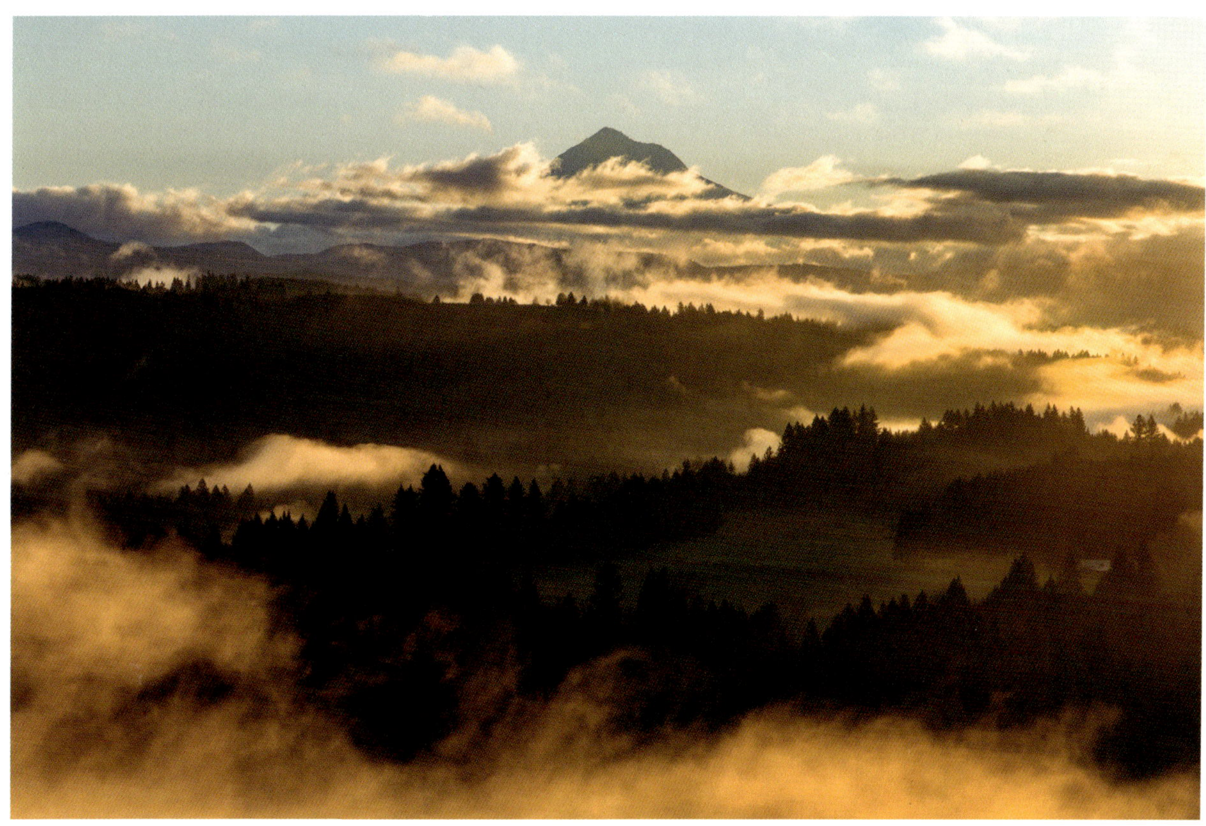



Mount Hood and Sandy River Valley from Jonsrud Viewpoint.
*Photo by Vldn Taylor*

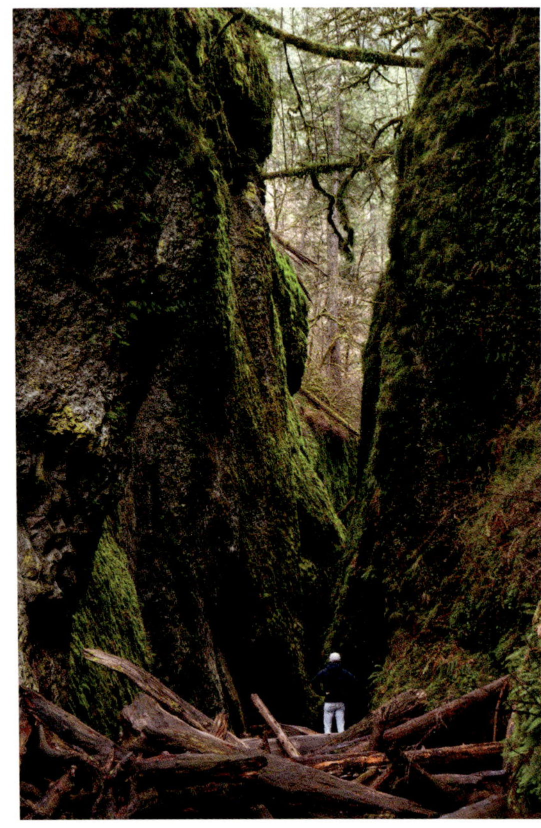

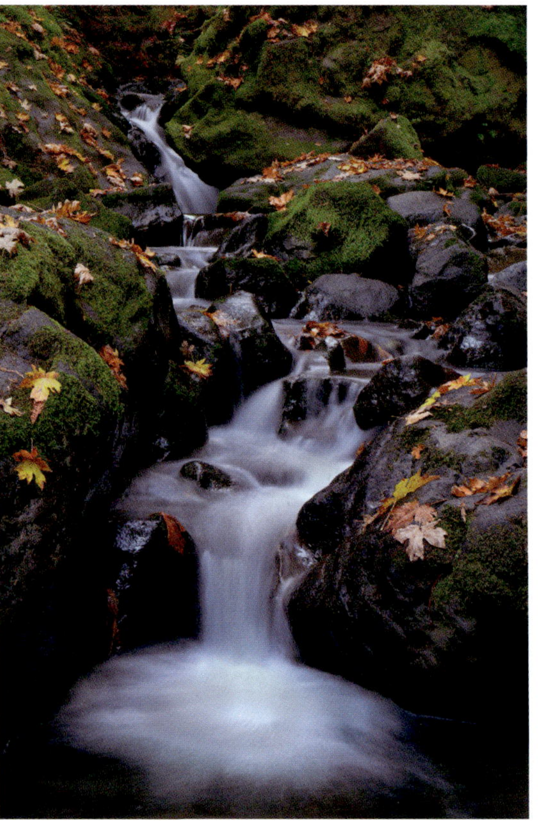

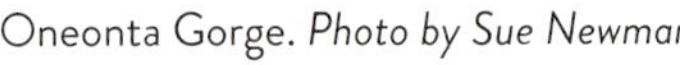
Oneonta Gorge. *Photo by Sue Newman*

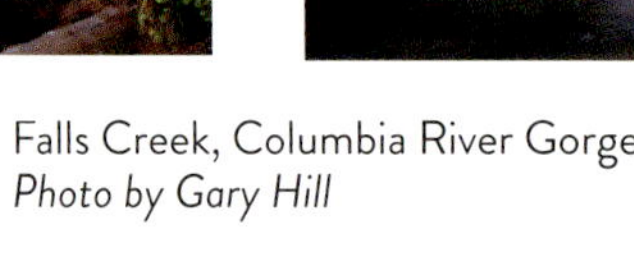
Falls Creek, Columbia River Gorge. *Photo by Gary Hill*

Tanner Creek, Columbia River Gorge. *Photo by Clem Paslack*

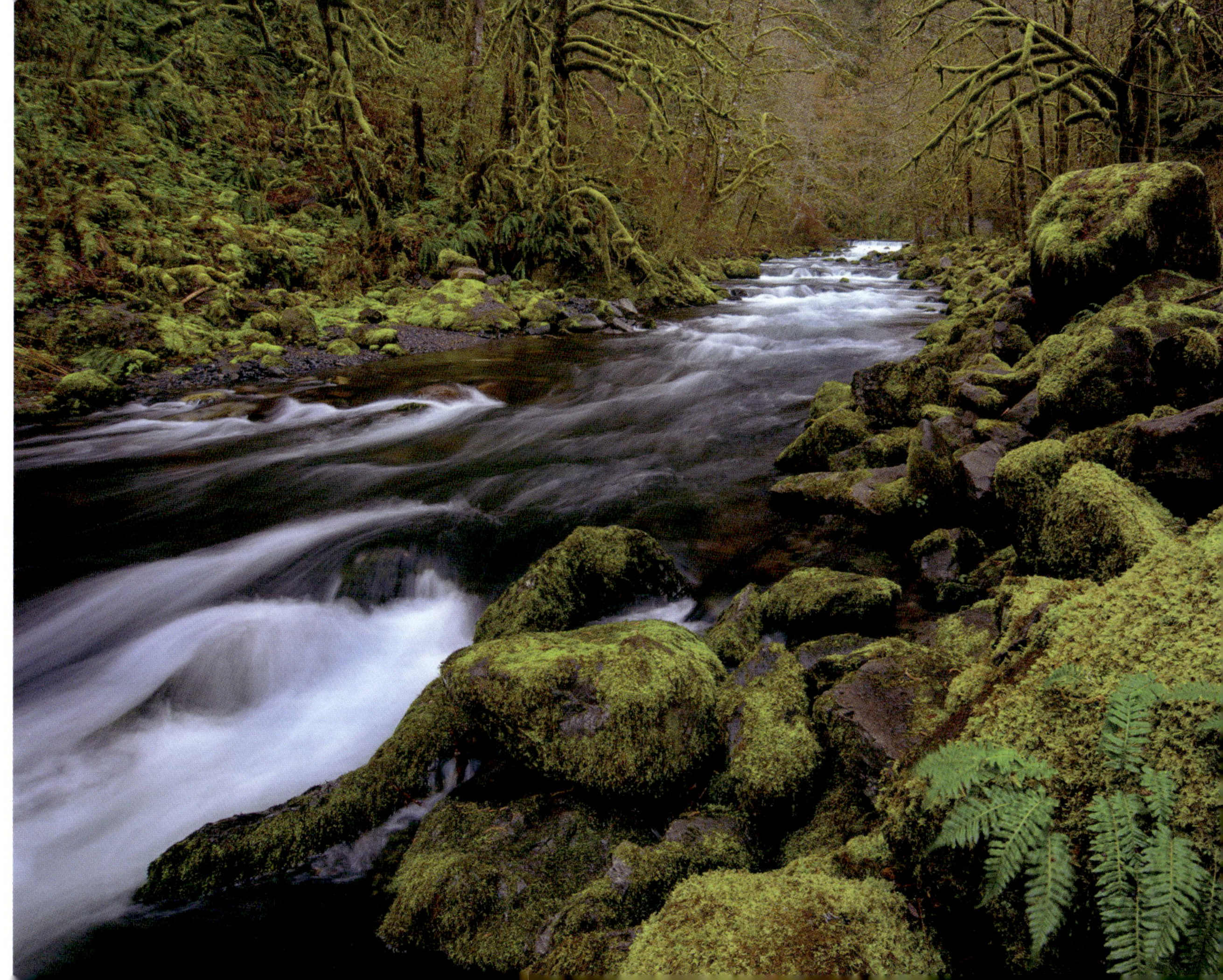

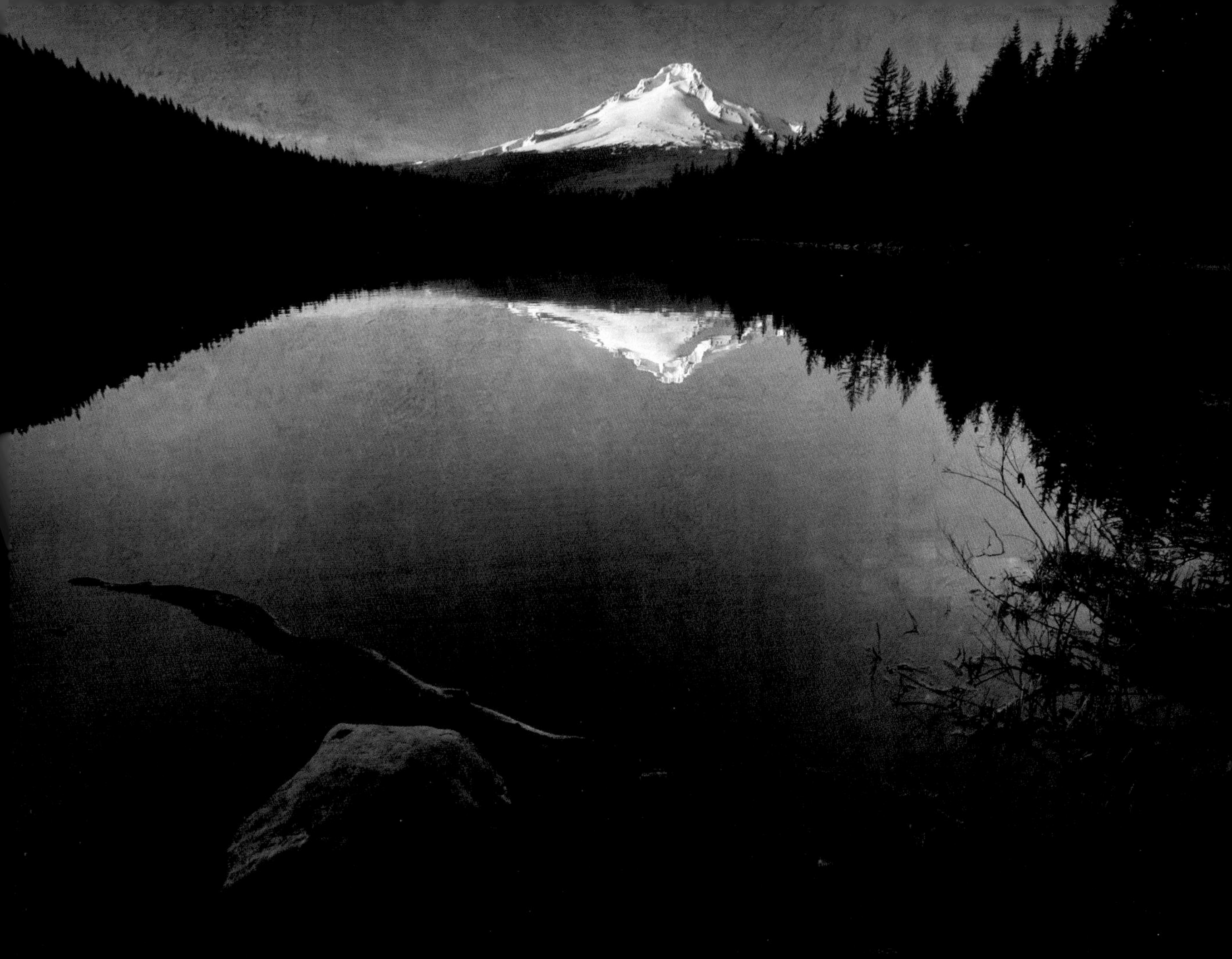

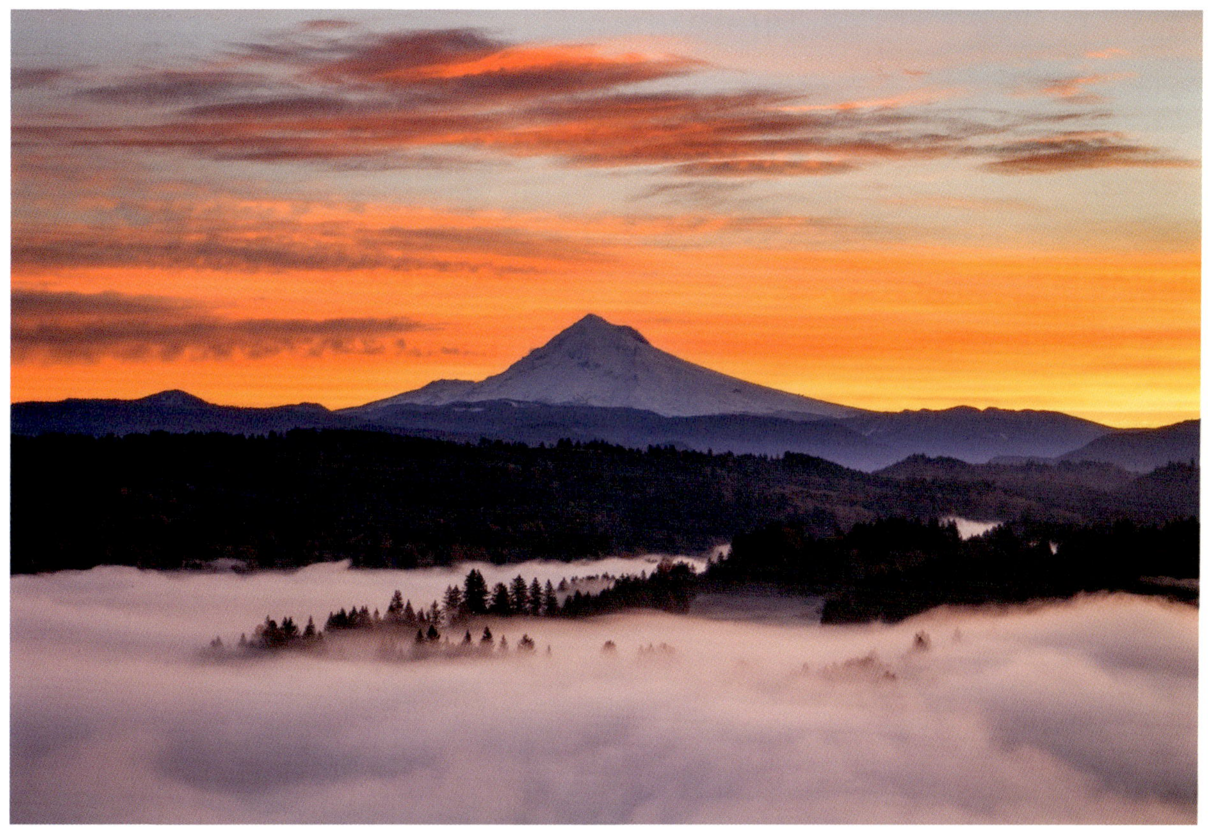

83

Trillium Lake and Mount Hood. *Photo by John Kirk*

Mount Hood, Jonsrud Viewpoint, Sandy. *Photo by Vldn Taylor*

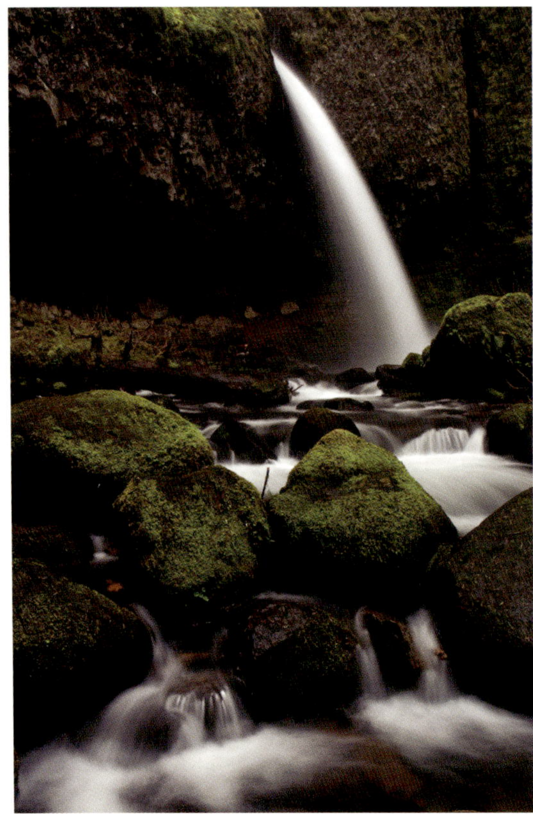

Ponytail Falls. *Photo by Jay Newman*

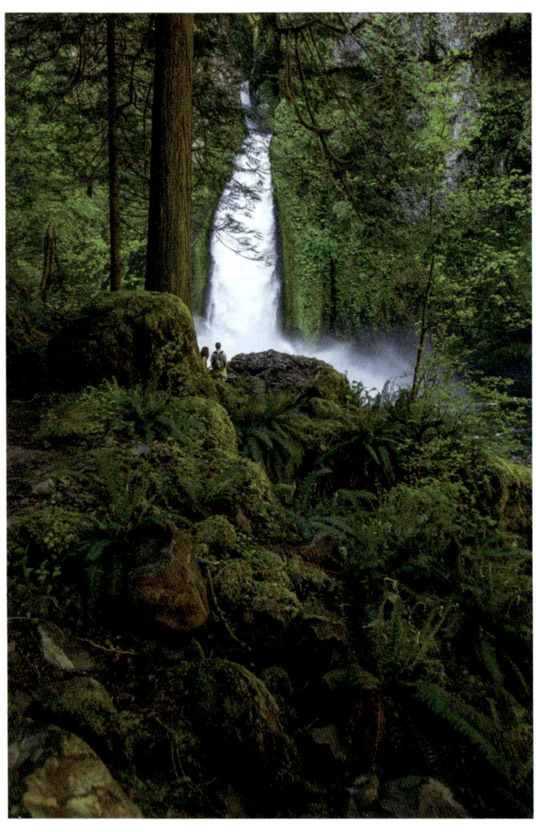

Wahclella Falls. *Photo by Kate Geary*

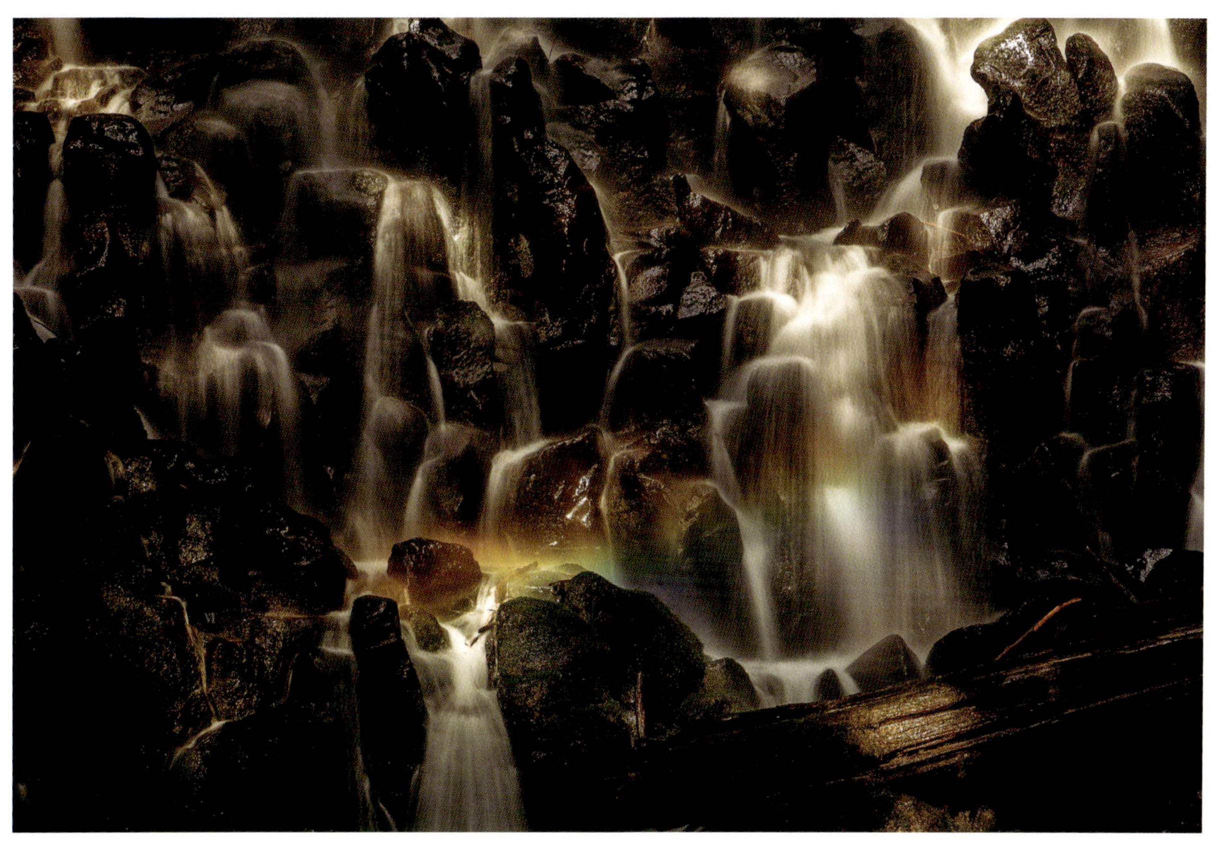

Ramona Falls. *Photo by Vldn Taylor*

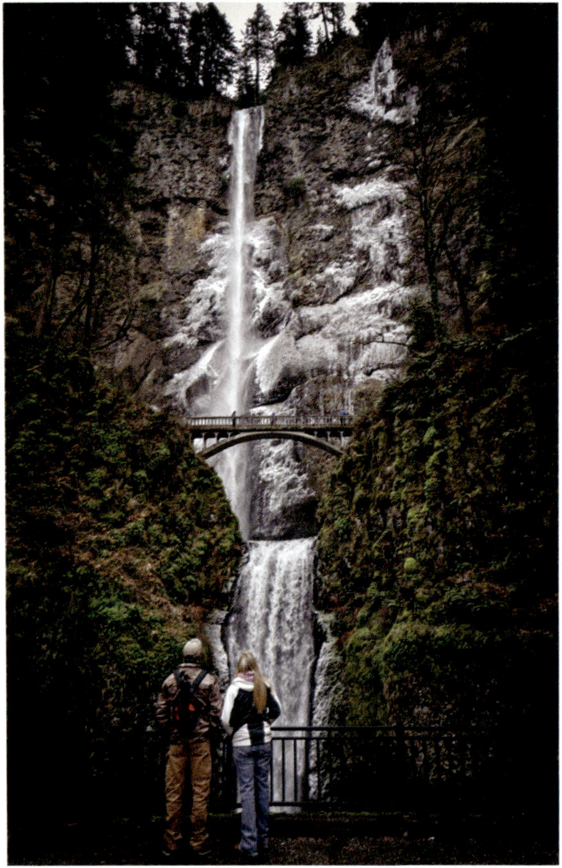

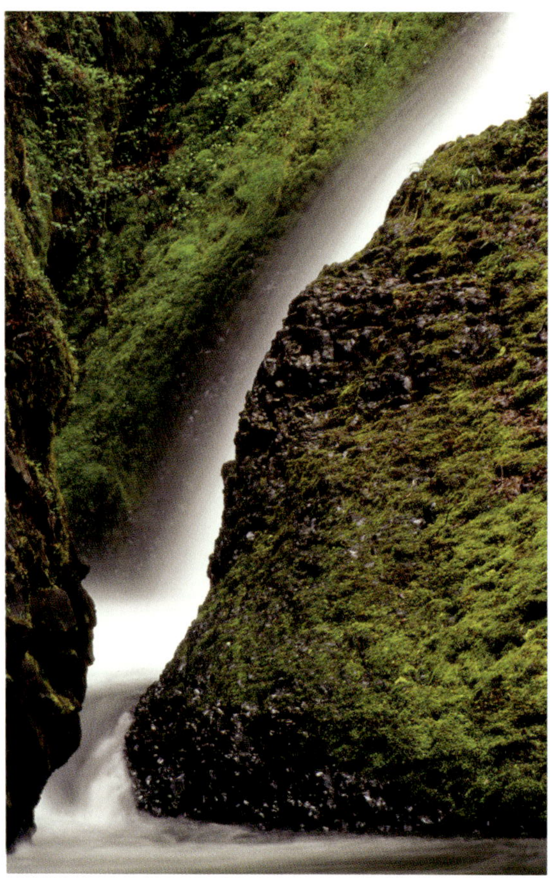

Multnomah Falls. *Photo by Barbara Tricarico*

Horsetail Falls. *Photo by Jay Newman*

Latourelle Falls. *Photo by Alana Lynn Starkweather*

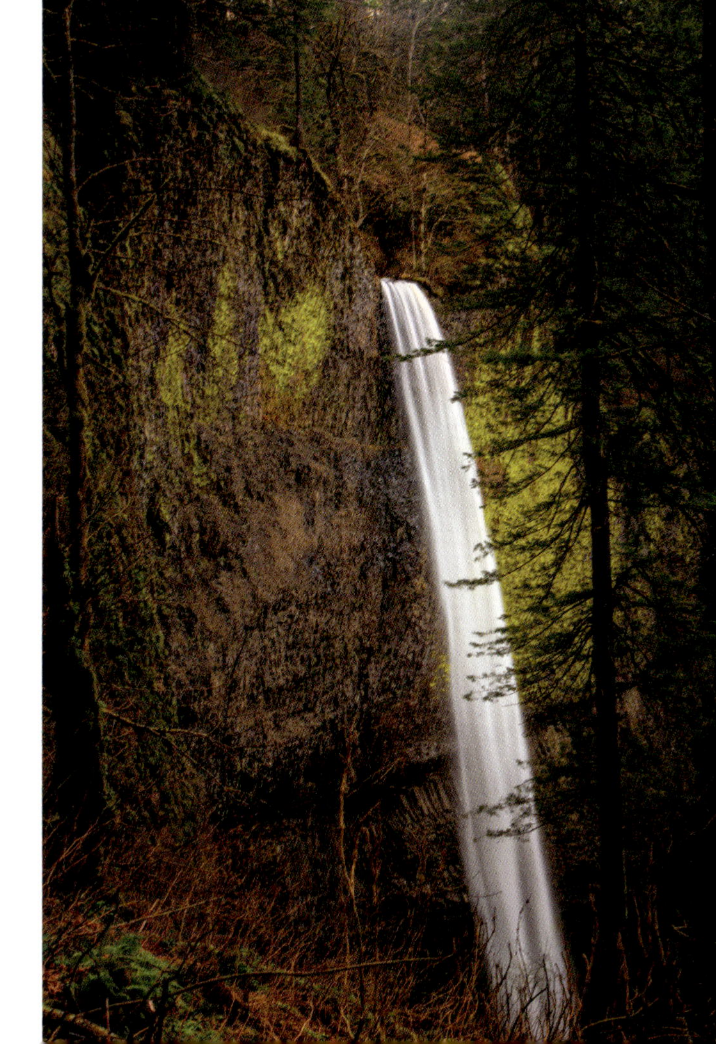

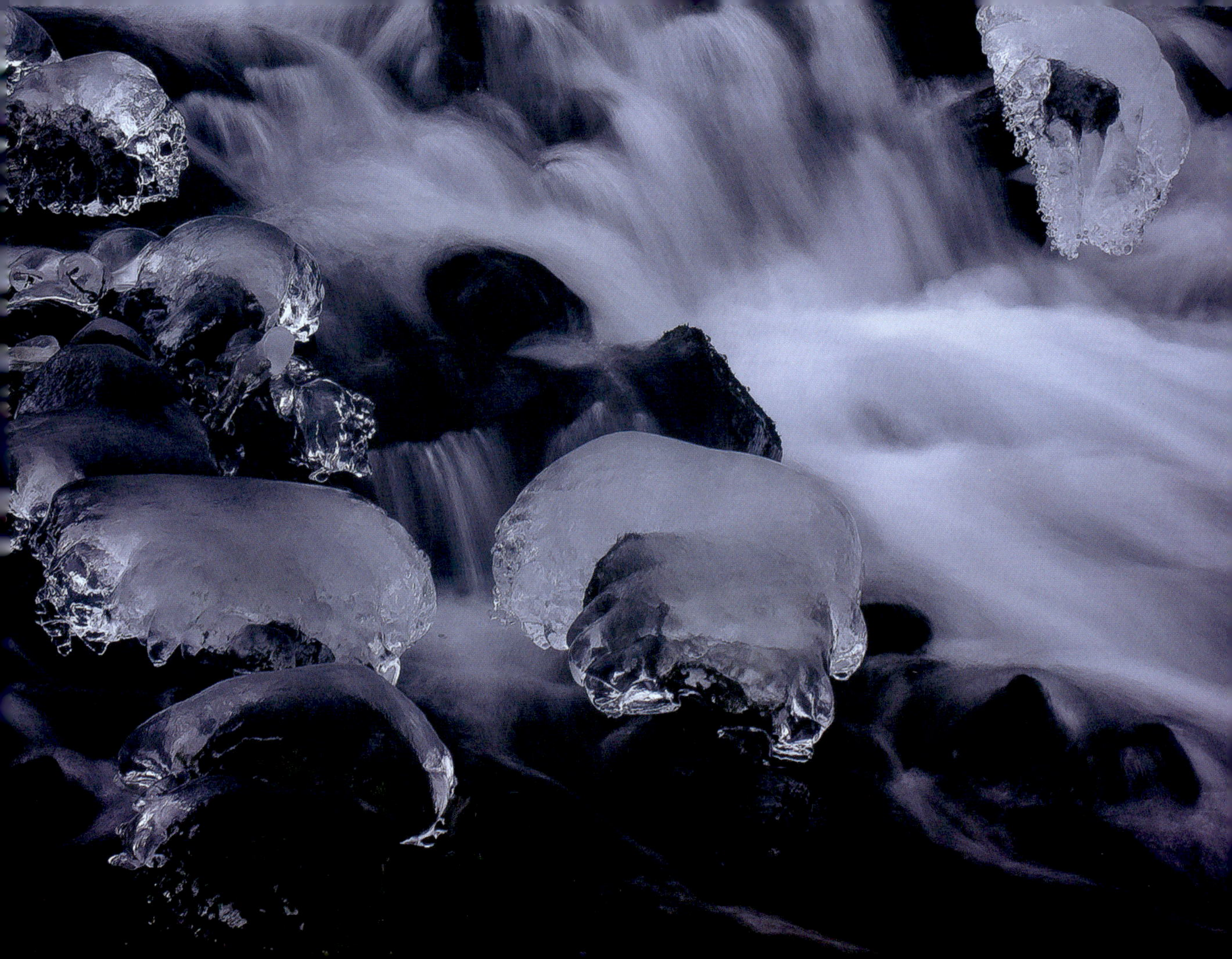

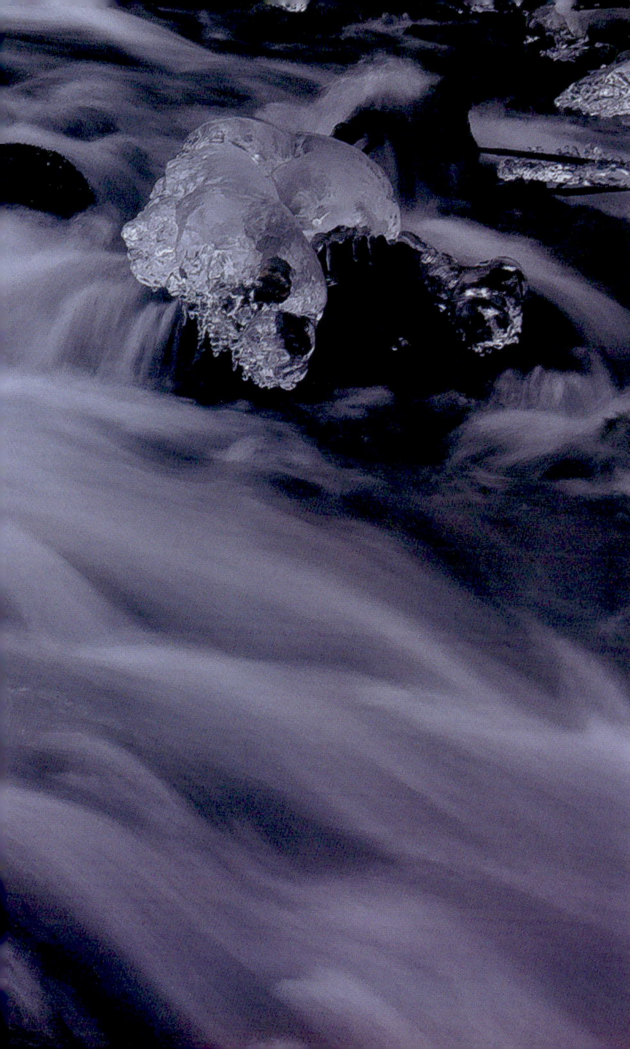



Columbia River Gorge ice. *Photo by Clem Paslack*

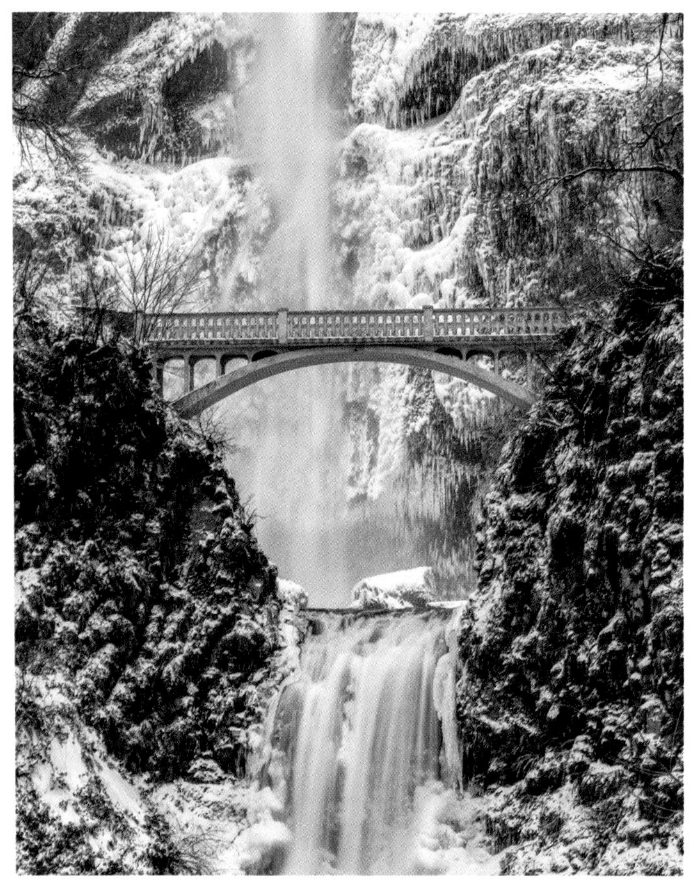

Multnomah Falls in winter. *Photo by Vldn Taylor*

Mount Hood, Trillium Lake. *Photo by Terry Tuttle*

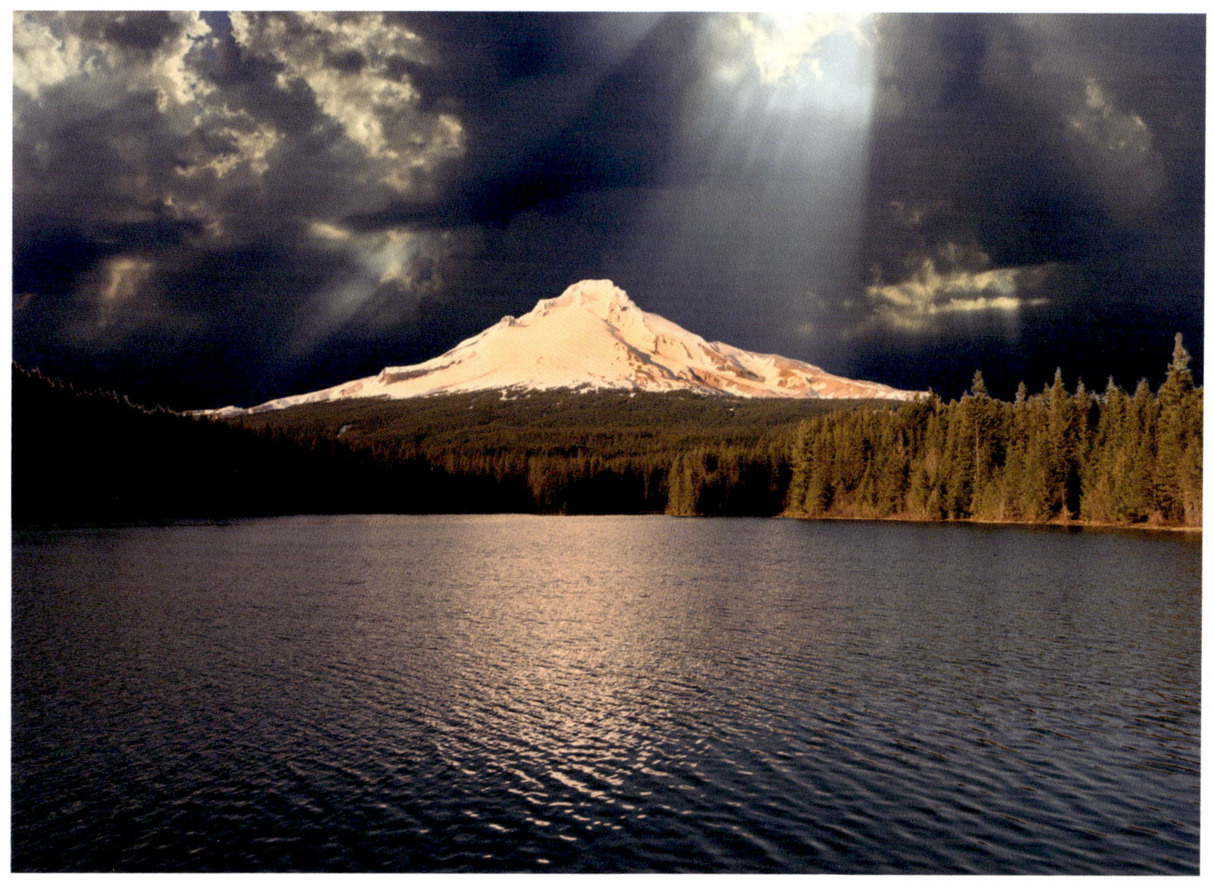

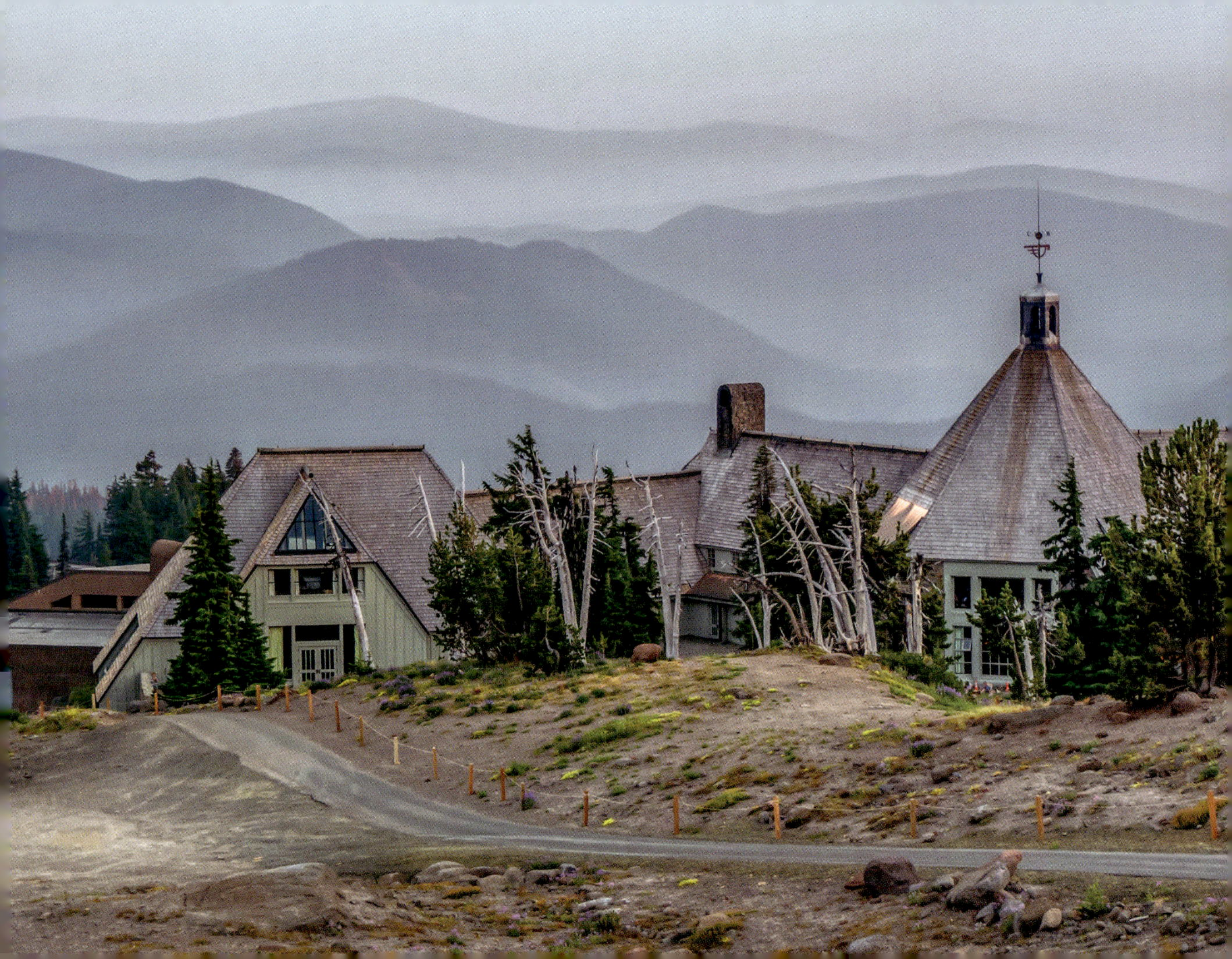

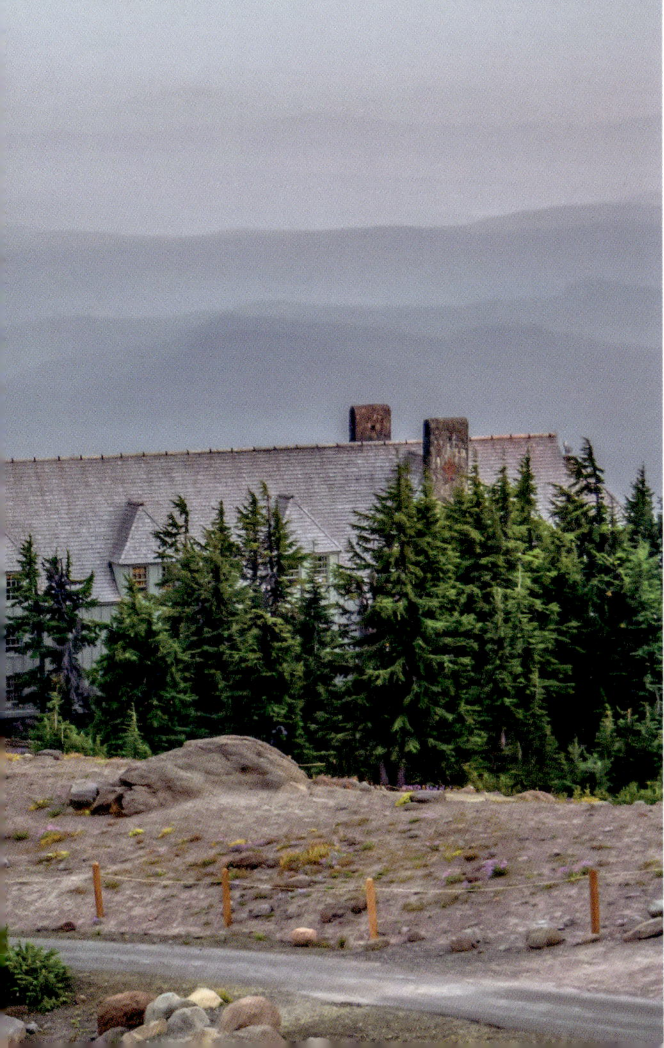



Timberline Lodge, Mount Hood, constructed by the Works Progress Administration in the 1930s. *Photo by Randy Bryan*

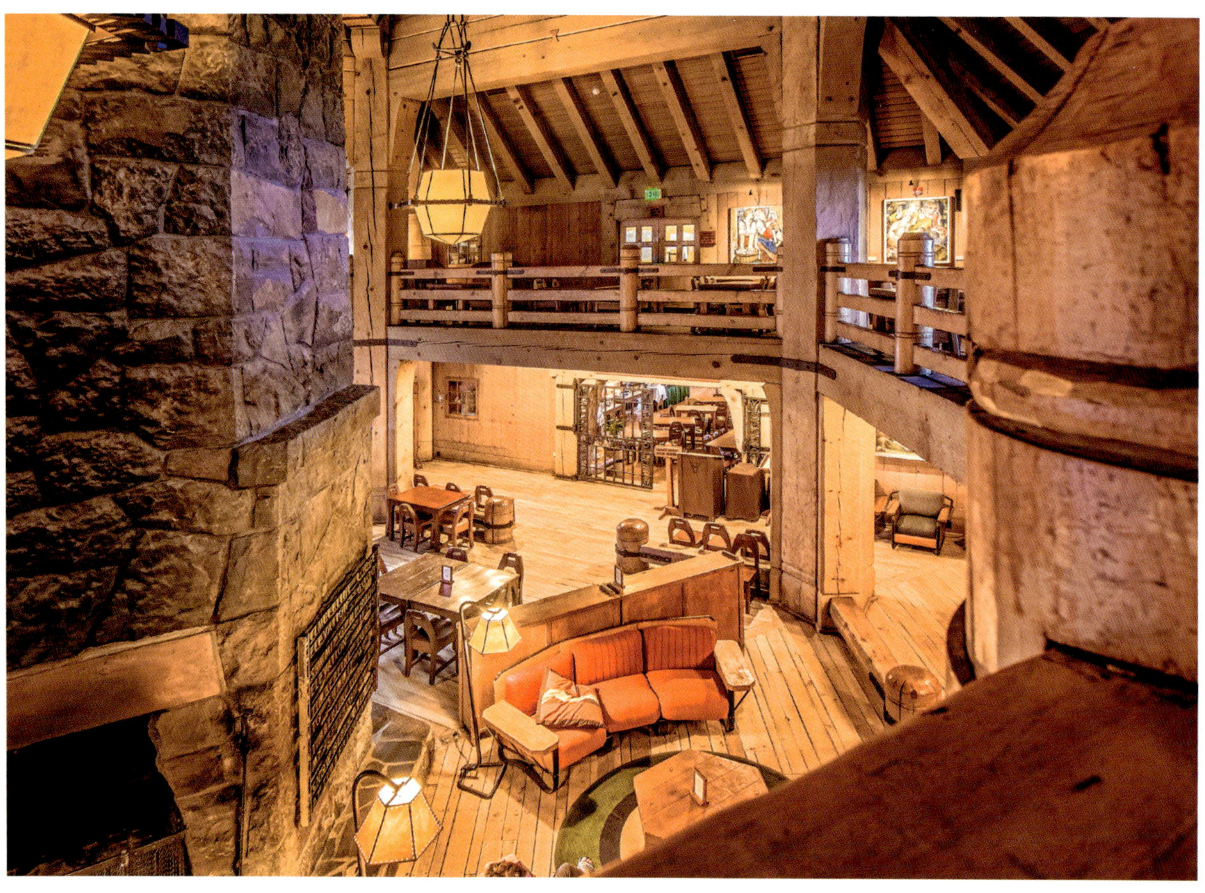

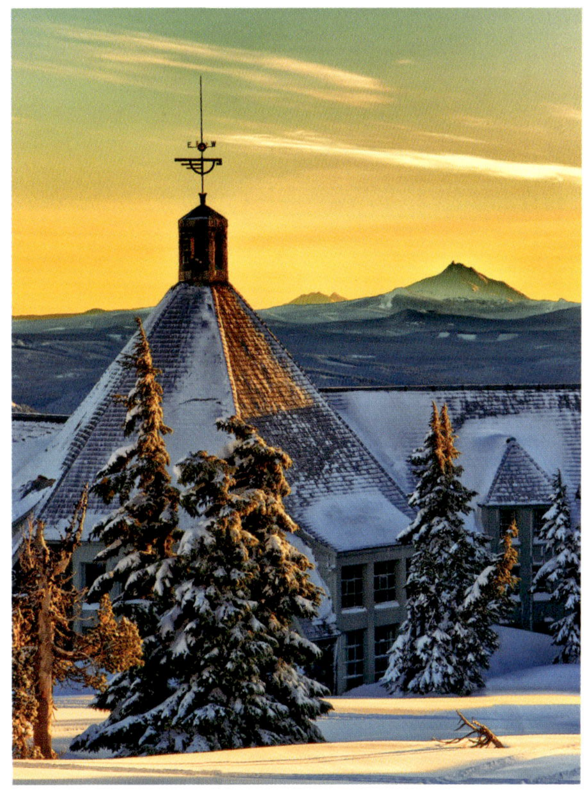

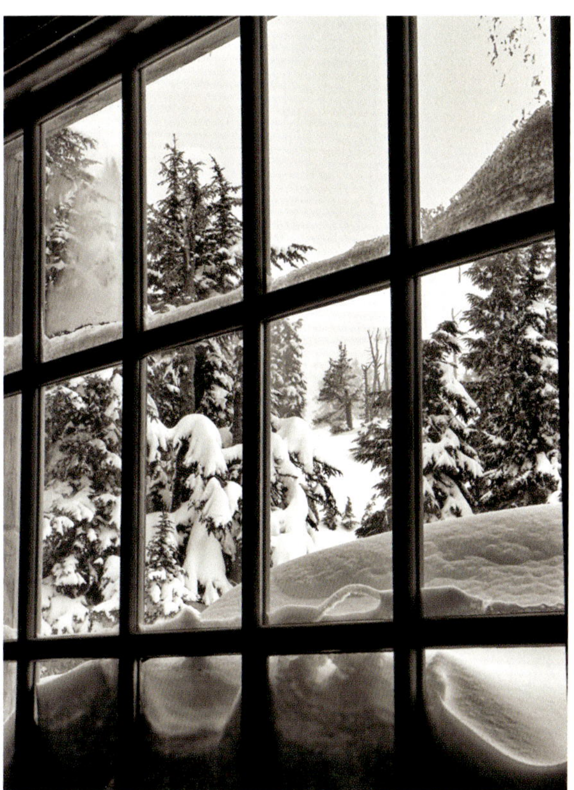

Timberline Lodge interior. Local artisans furnished the lodge during the Great Depression. *Photo by Randy Bryan*

Timberline Lodge, Mount Hood. The lodge was constructed from 1936 to 1938. *Photo by Vivian McAleavey*

View from Timberline Lodge. *Photo by Vivian McAleavey*

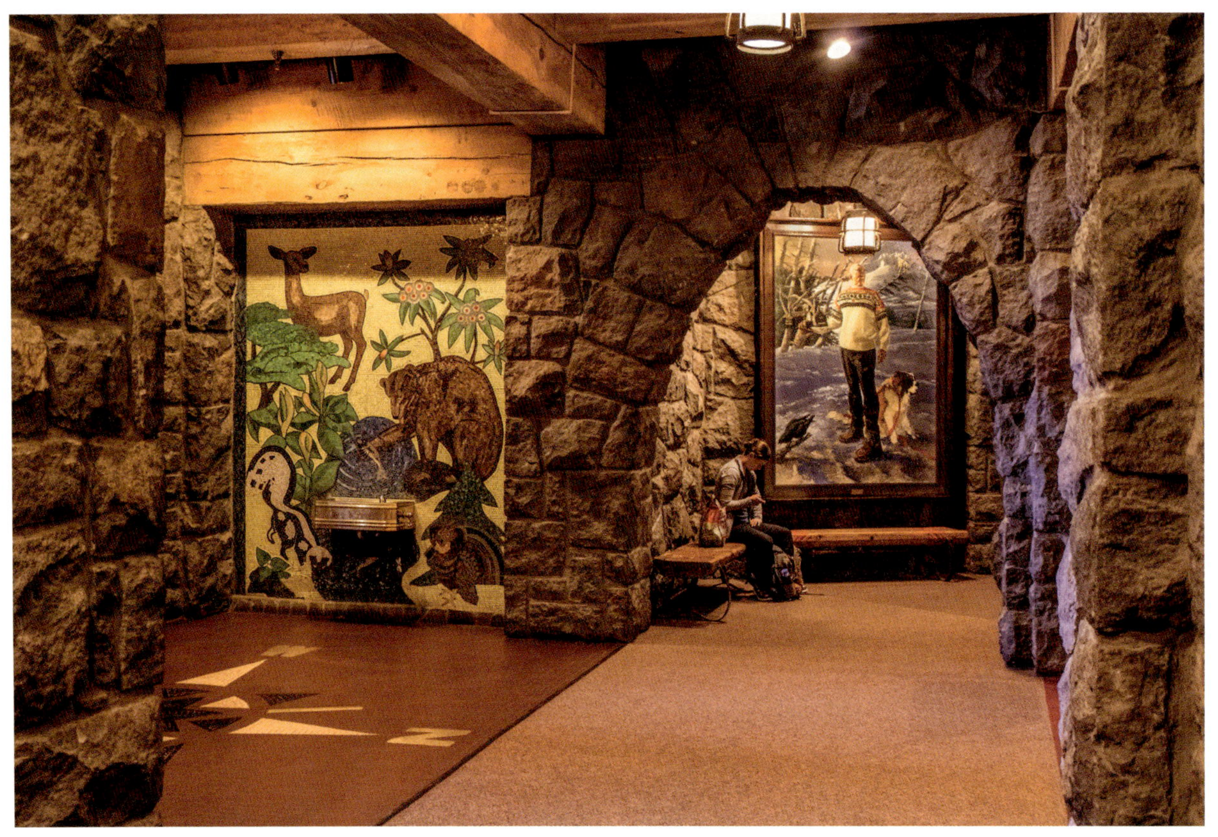

Timberline Lodge interior. President Franklin D. Roosevelt dedicated the lodge in 1937. *Photo by George F. Peterson*

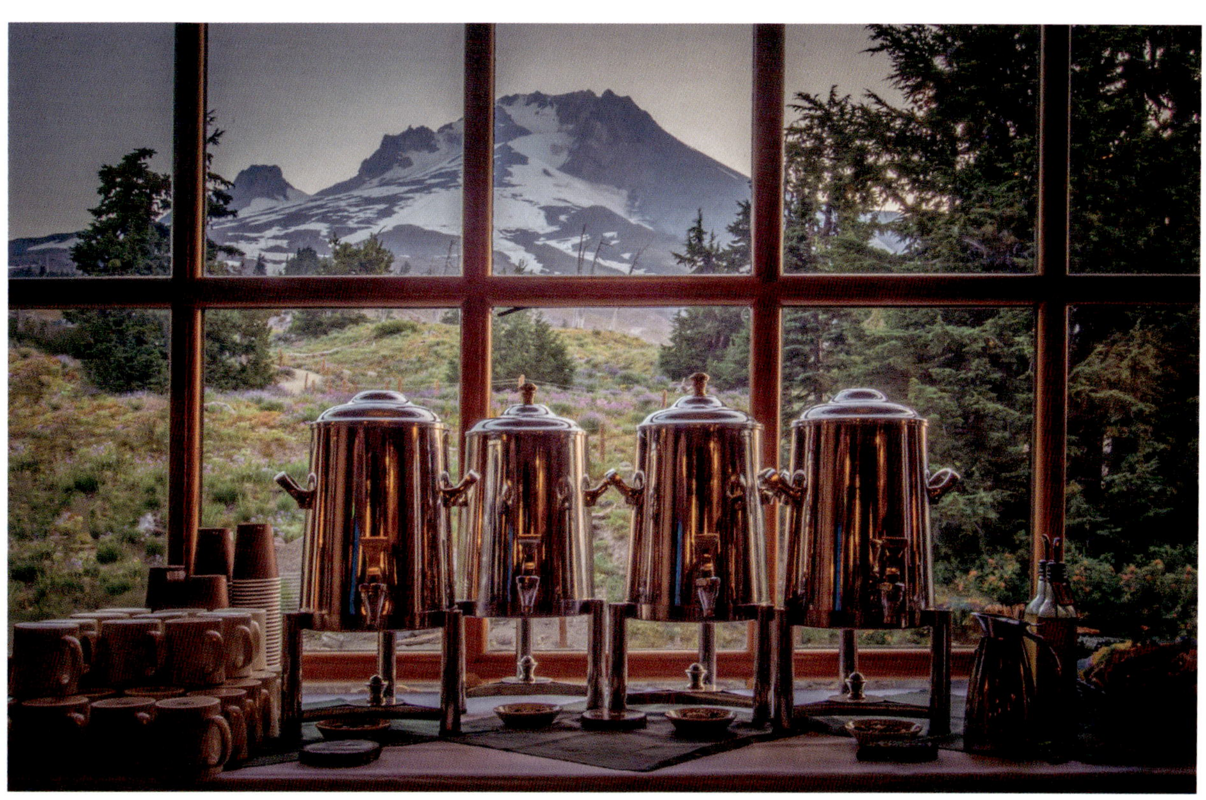



View of Mount Hood from interior of Timberline Lodge.
*Photo by Randy Bryan*

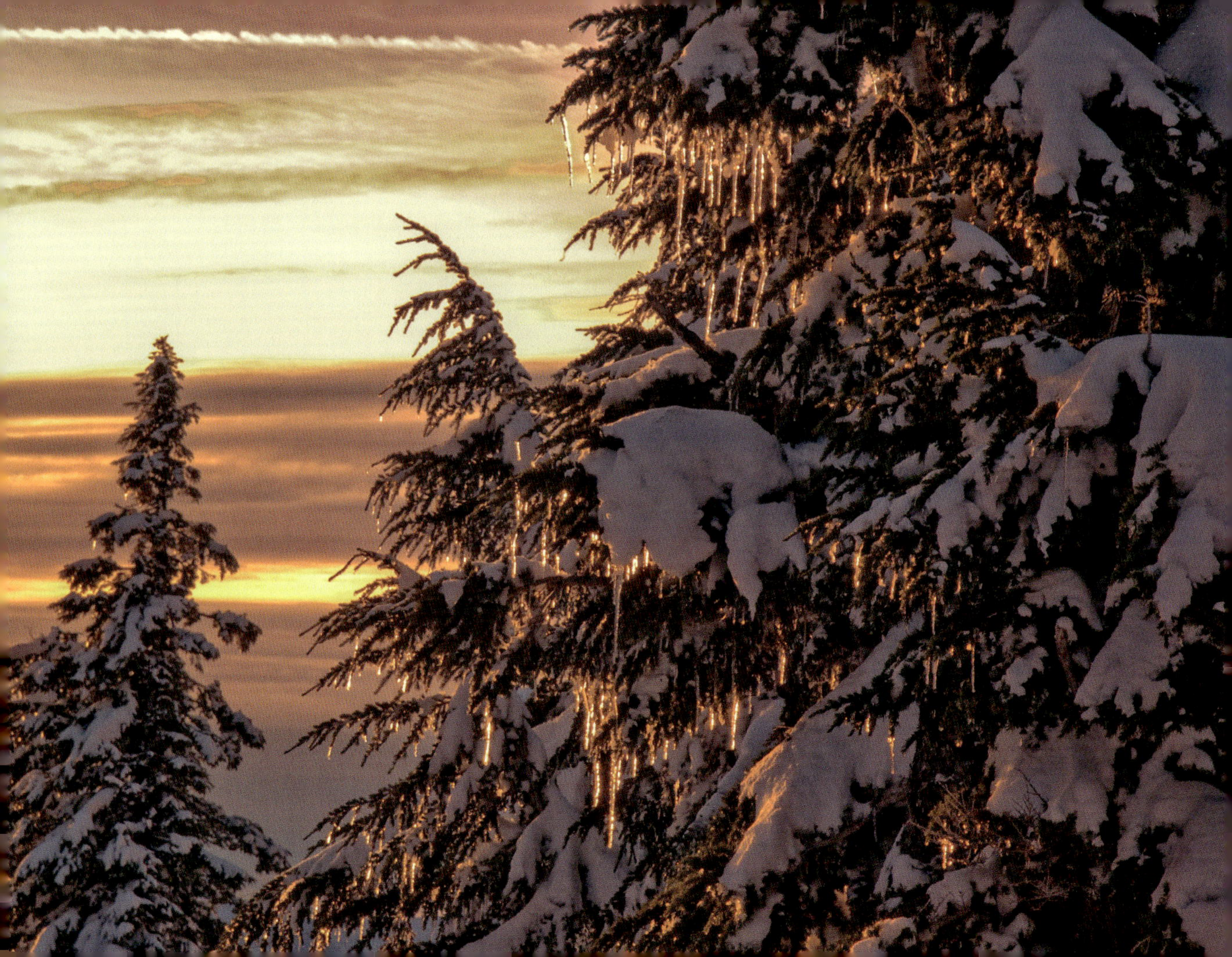

Sunrise at Mount Hood.
*Photo by Vivian McAleavey*

Skiing at Mount Hood.
*Photo by Vldn Taylor*

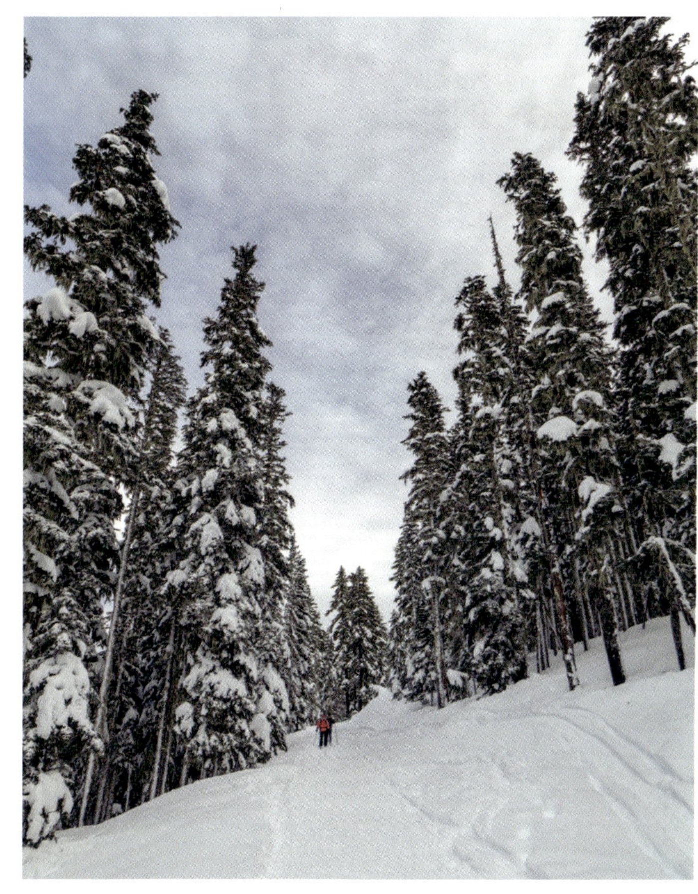

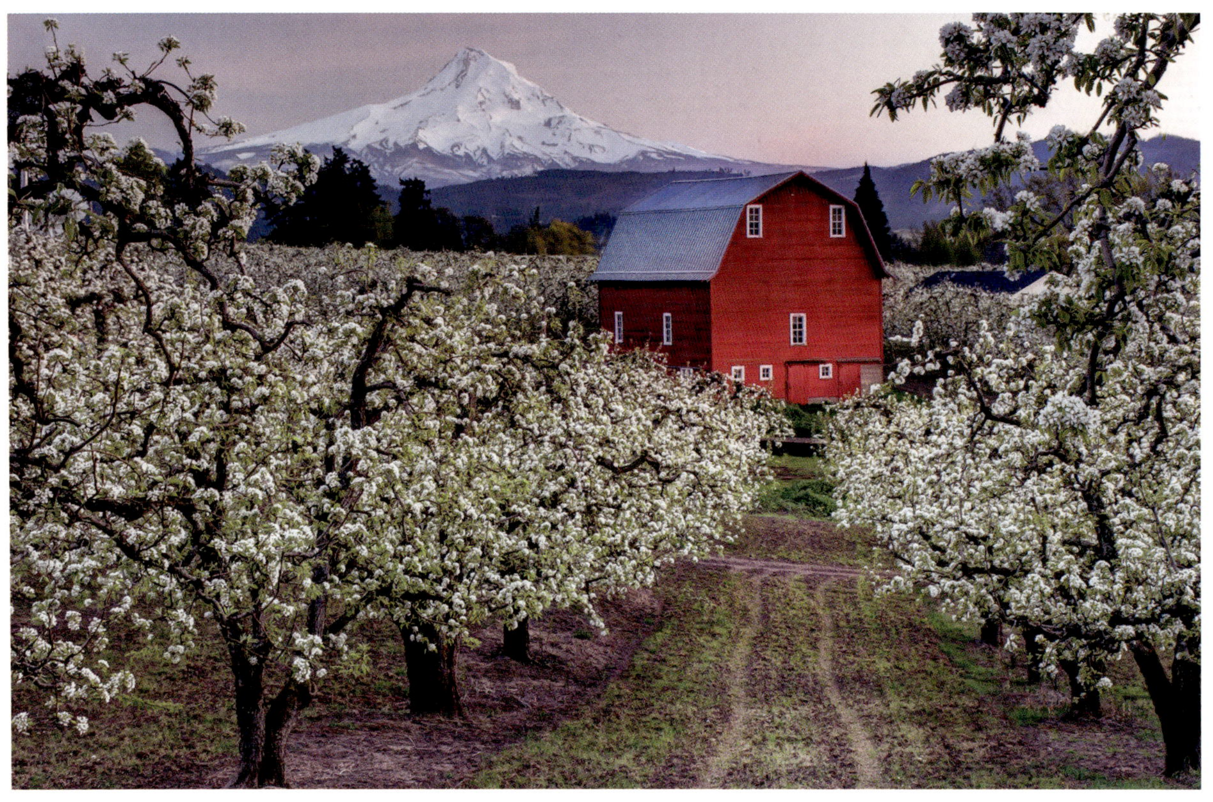

Orchard blossoms near Hood River. *Photo by Clem Paslack*

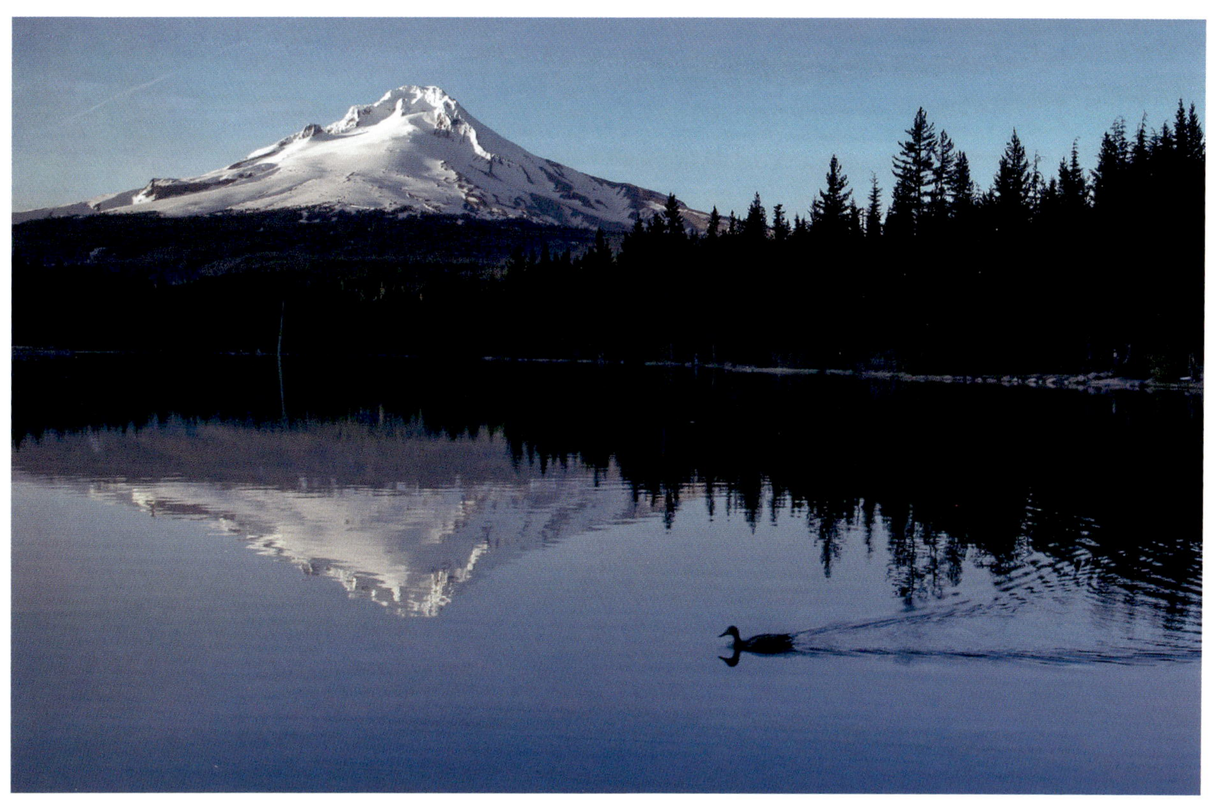



Trillium Lake and Mount Hood. *Photo by John Kirk*

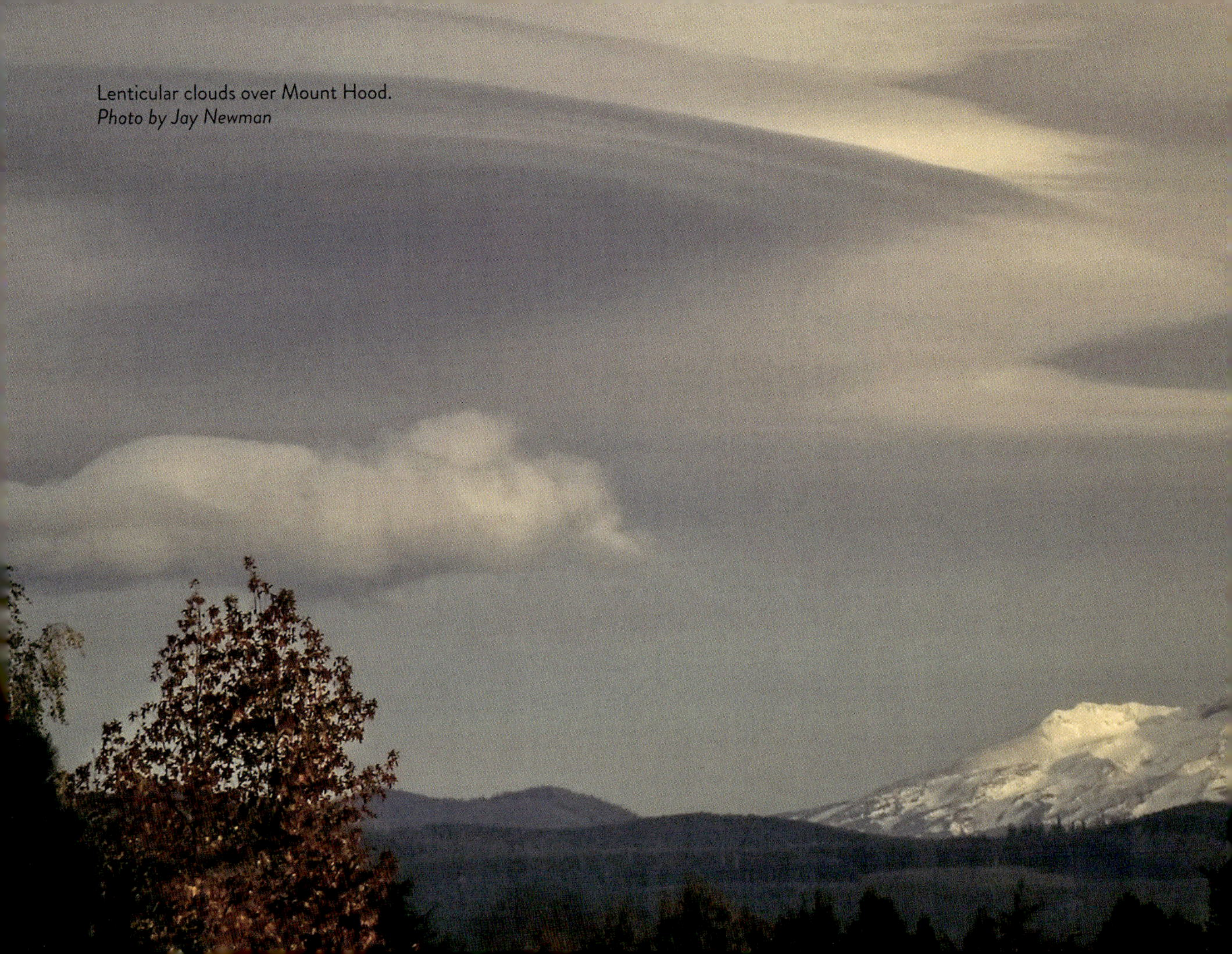

Lenticular clouds over Mount Hood.
*Photo by Jay Newman*

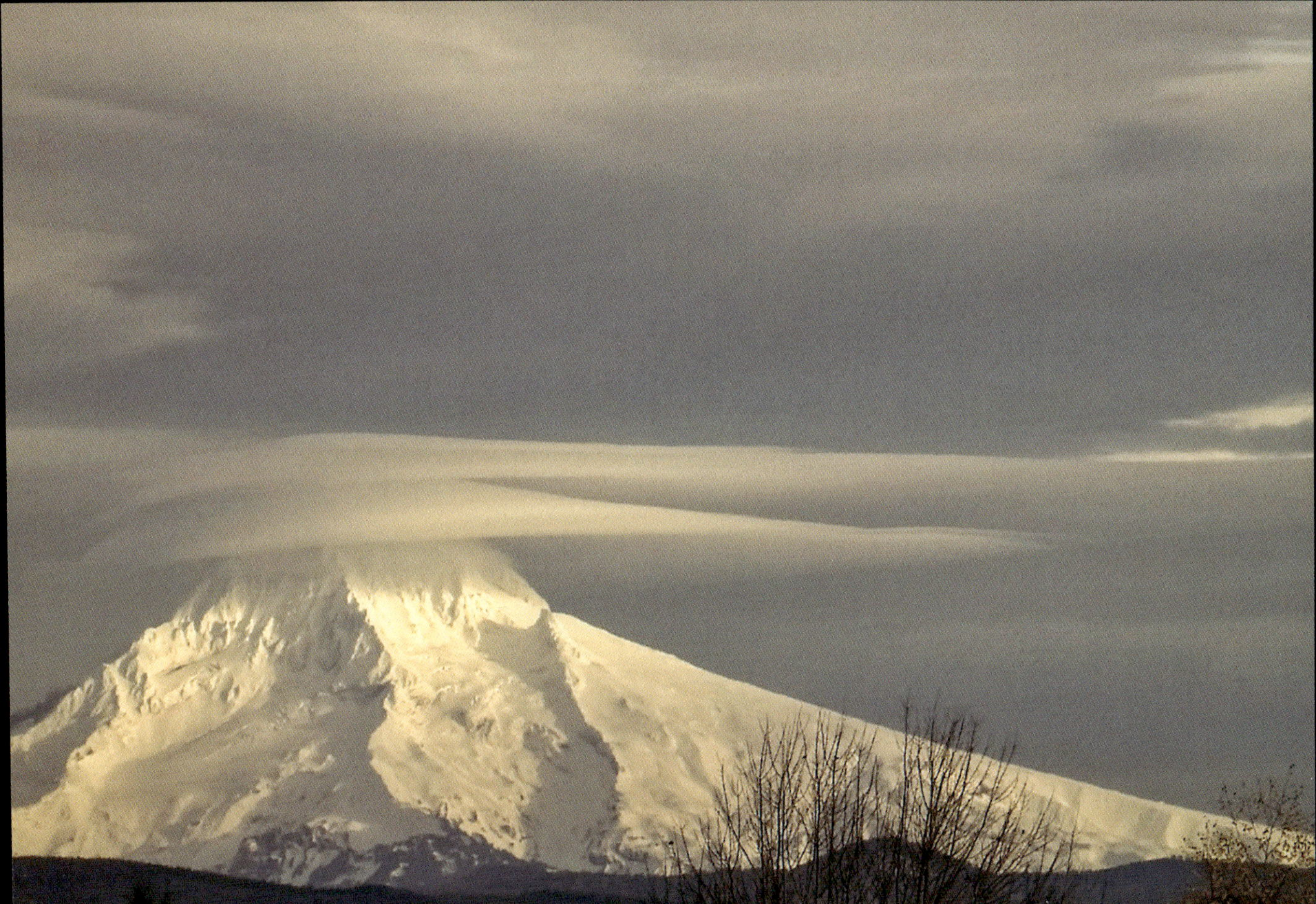

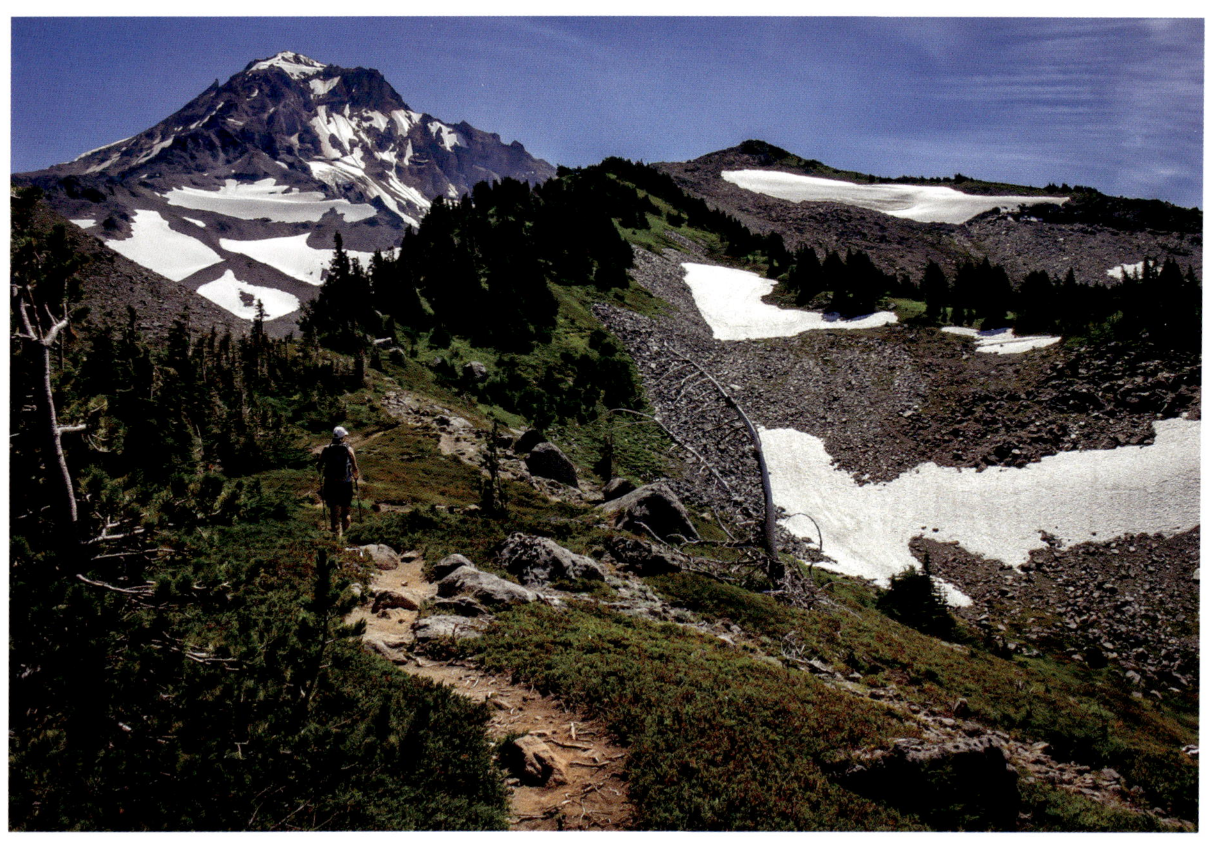

Hiking Mount Hood. *Photo by Gary Hill*

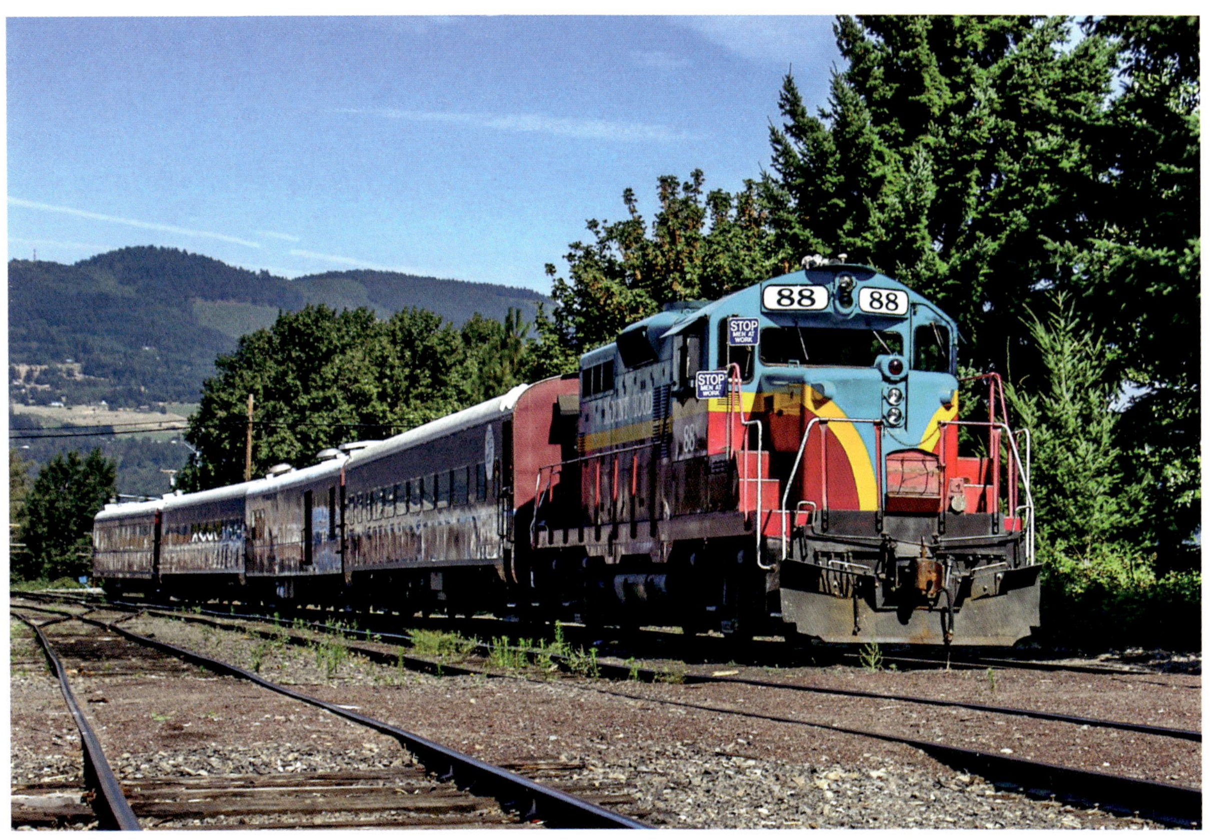


Mount Hood Railroad is a tourist railroad operating between Hood River and Parkdale. It began operating in 1906. *Photo by George F. Peterson*

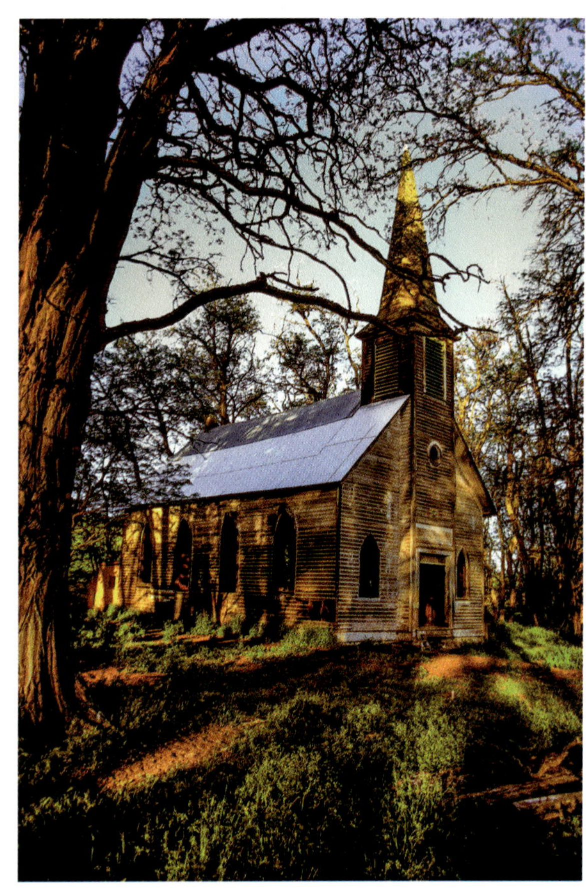

Old church, Wildwood, Mount Hood National Forest. *Photo by Neal R. Thompson*

Apple orchards in Hood River. *Photo by John Kirk*

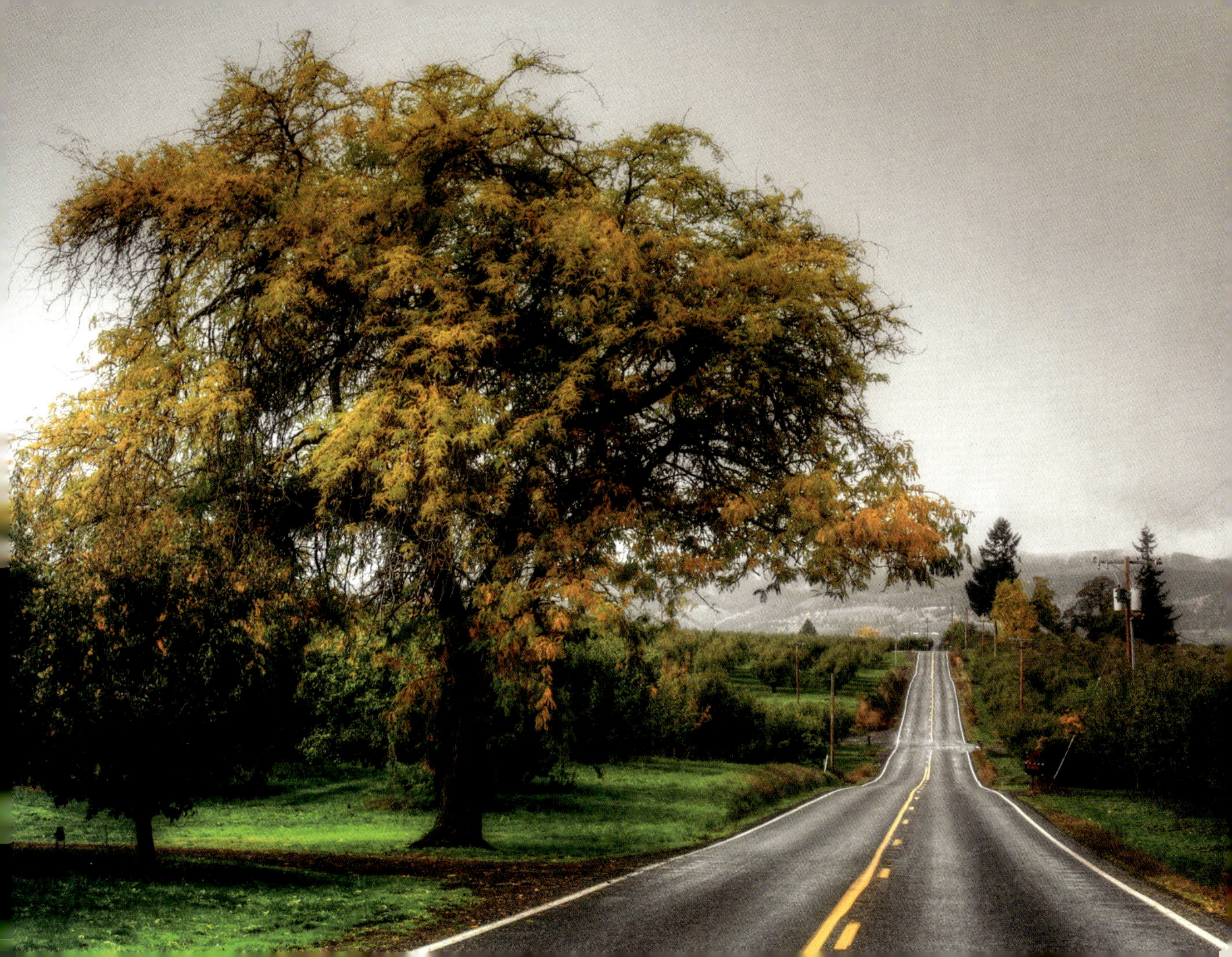

108

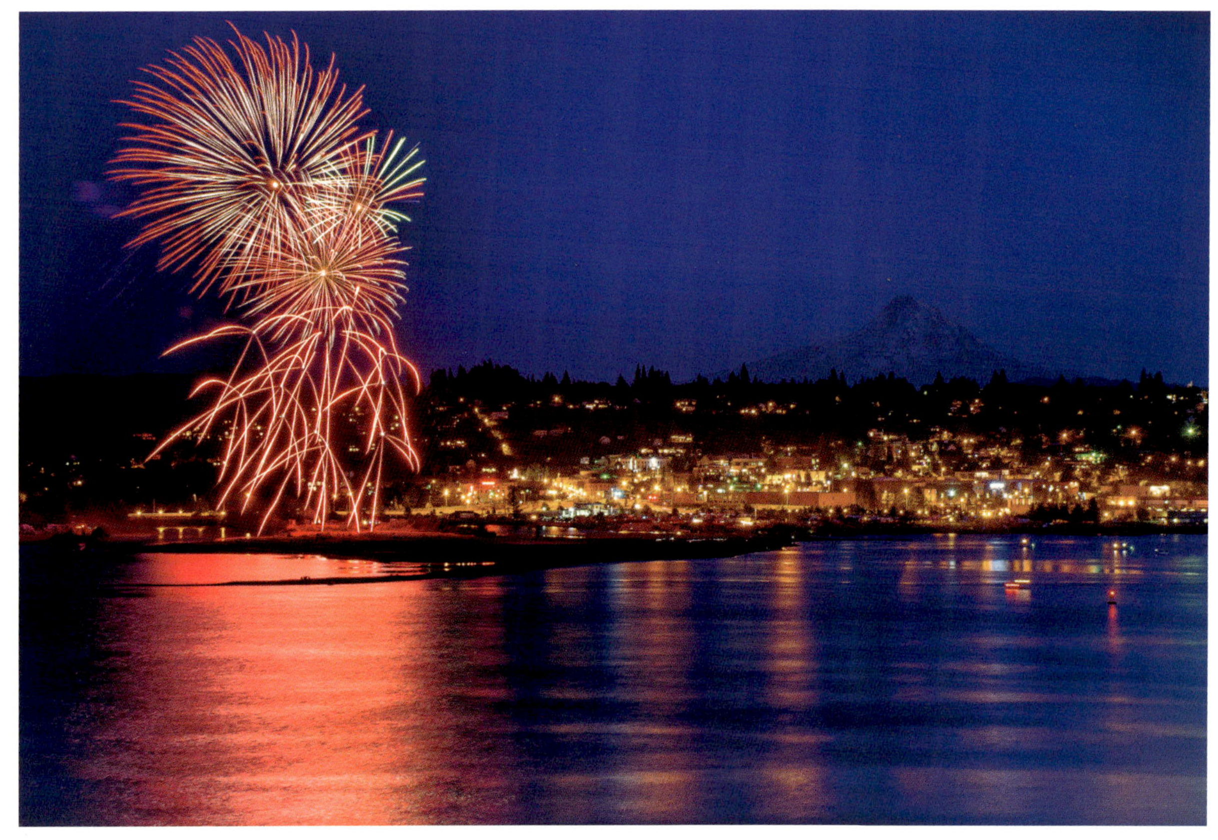

July 4th fireworks at Hood River. Mount Hood in background.
*Photo by Clem Paslack*

Rowena Crest Viewpoint, Columbia River Gorge.
*Photo by Clem Paslack*

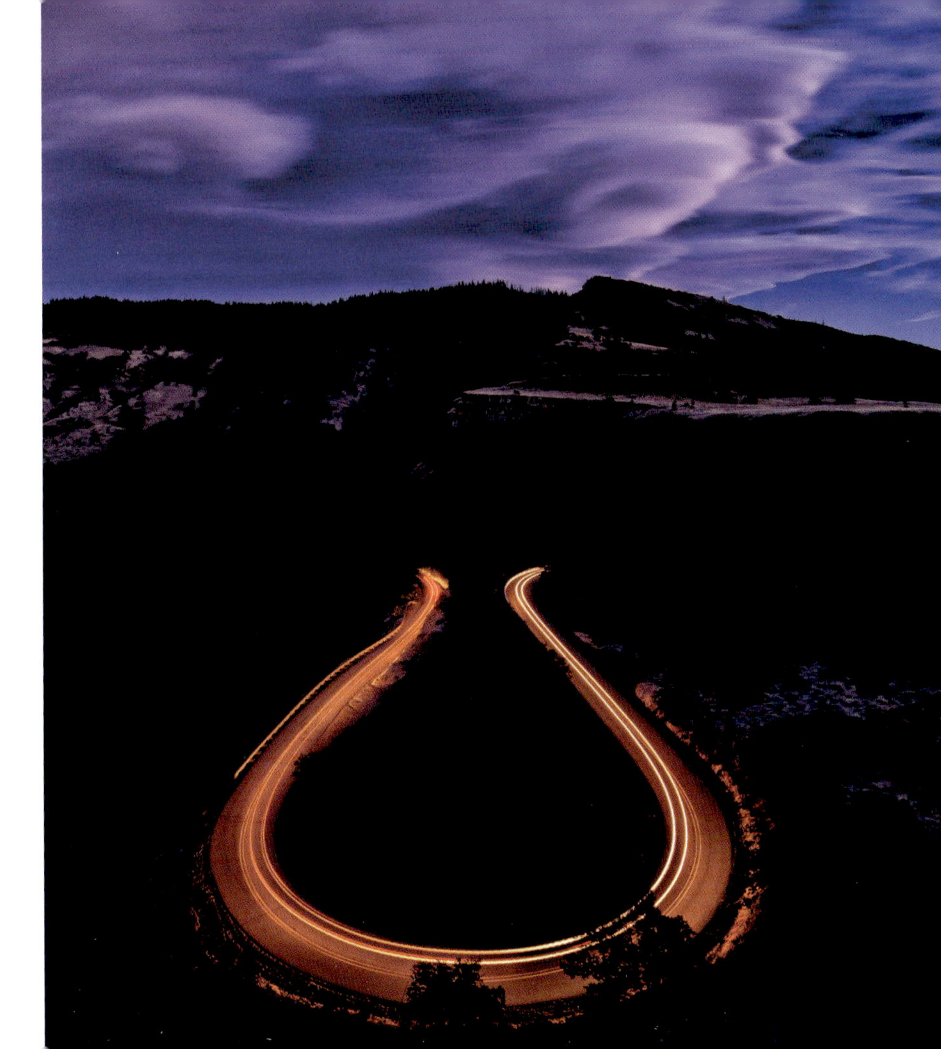

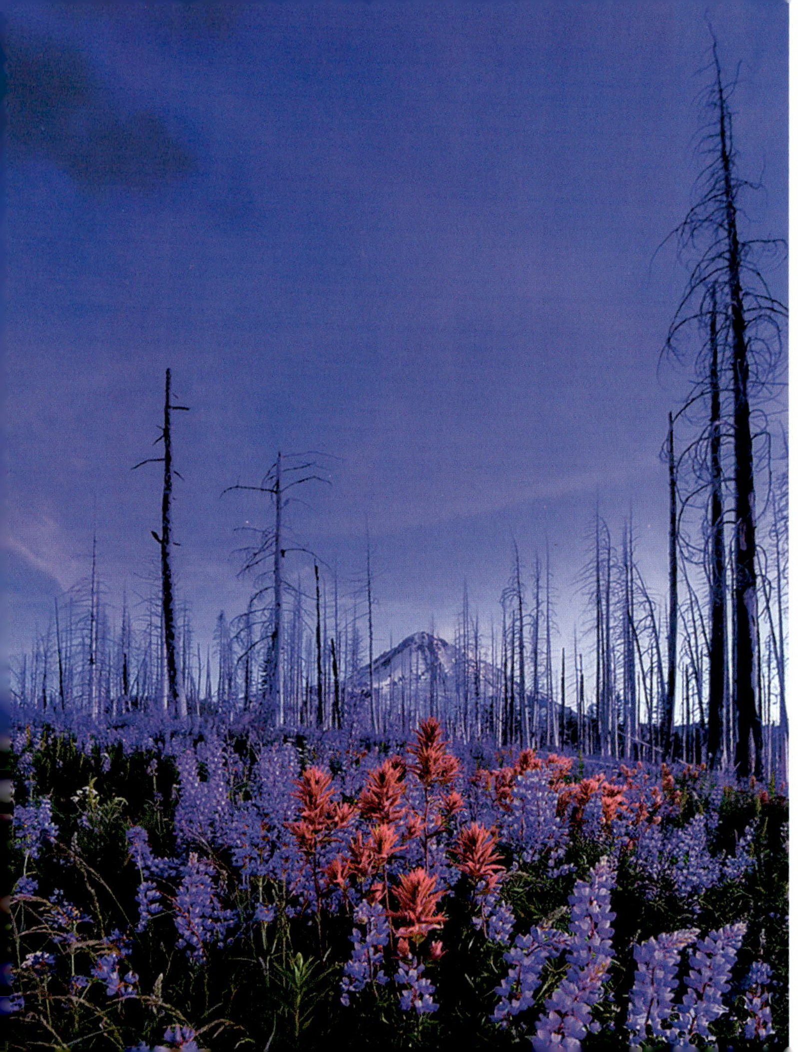

Mount Hood forest rebirth.
*Photo by Clem Paslack*

# CREDITS

Thank you to the following Oregon photographers who contributed to this book:

Randy Bryan
Dan Elster
Terry Fisher
Kate Geary
Nomeca Hartwell
Gary Hill
Charles Hillestad
John Kirk
Geri H. Mathewson
Cornelius Matteo
Vivian McAleavey
Tysen Mueller
Jay Newman
Sue Newman
Bob Palermini
Clem Paslack
George F. Peterson
Diana Standing
Alana Lynn Starkweather
Hans Stroo
Vldn Taylor
Neal R. Thompson
Barbara Tricarico
Terry Tuttle
Nick Viani

*Author photo credit:*
*Cornelius Matteo*

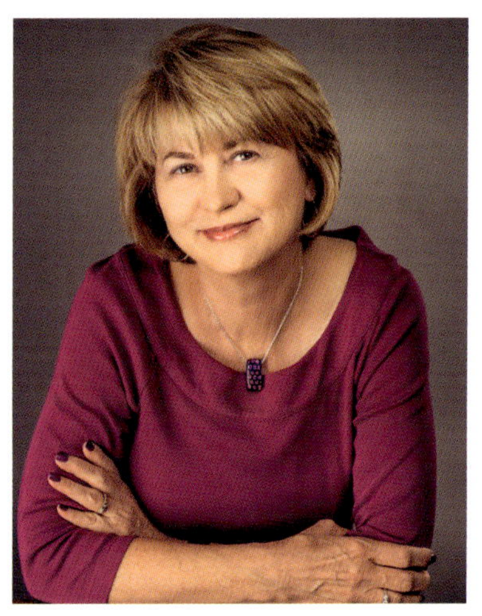

**Barbara Tricarico** has produced nine Oregon photography books by Schiffer, including three coffee-table books: *Oregon*; *Ashland, Oregon*; and *Ashland, Oregon Day Trips*, as well as coauthoring and photographing *Quilts of Virginia: 1607–1899*. She and her husband, Bill, moved to Ashland, Oregon, in 2010. Barbara is an active member of the Ashland Chamber of Commerce and Southern Oregon Photographic Association. She is a regular volunteer for the Ashland Food Project and the Oregon Shakespeare Festival. Barbara has traveled and photographed extensively around the world. Follow her on Facebook at Barbara Tricarico Photography or visit her website, www.barbaratricarico.com.